- The Treaty establishing a Constitution for Europe was signed in Rome on 29 October 2004 by the Heads of State or Government of the twenty-five Member States.

- The European Constitution will come into force on 1 November 2006 if it is ratified by the 25 Member States of the European Union, either in parliament or by referendum.

- In January 2005, the European Parliament voted in favour of the Treaty establishing a Constitution for Europe by 500 votes to 137, with 40 abstentions.

Dear European citizens,

The European Parliament is delighted to welcome you here today as one of the thousands of visitors we receive every year.

I hope your visit to our institution will give you an insight into the day-to-day work of the MEPs you have elected.

Your visit comes at a time when the European Union is preparing to adopt a Constitution and when the European Parliament has given its overwhelming backing to the project by approving the Corbett – Méndez de Vigo report.

Marking a major step towards a political Europe, this Constitution is first and foremost about you. It enshrines your fundamental rights, both civil and political, and the democratic values on which the European Union is founded. Furthermore, it provides the basis for the European Union to speak with a single voice in the world.

If it is ratified by the national parliaments or by the people of the 25 Member States its adoption will consolidate our 50 years of European history and lead our Union into a stage of maturity.

This publication aims to provide you with all the information you need to participate actively in a debate which will determine the future of the Union and, therefore, your future.

Josep BORRELL FONTELLES
President of the European Parliament

CONTENTS

European Parliament resolution on the Treaty establishing a Constitution for Europe (2004/2129(INI))

The European Parliament,

- having regard to the Treaty establishing a Constitution for Europe (hereinafter 'the Constitution'),

- having regard to the Treaty on European Union and the Treaty establishing the European Community as amended by the Single European Act and the Treaties of Maastricht, Amsterdam and Nice,

- having regard to the Charter of Fundamental Rights of the European Union[1],

- having regard to the European Council's Laeken Declaration[2],

- having regard to its resolutions[3] paving the way towards a Constitution for Europe,

- having regard to its resolutions[4] preparing past intergovernmental conferences and its resolutions[5] assessing their outcome,
- having regard to the draft Treaty establishing a Constitution for Europe adopted by consensus by the European Convention on 13 June and 10 July 2003, as well as its resolutions[6] preparing and subsequently assessing the work of the Convention,

- having regard to the opinions on the Constitution delivered by the Committee of the Regions on 17 November 2004[7] and the European Economic and Social Committeeon 28 October 2004[8] at the request of the European Parliament[9],

- having regard to the views expressed by the representatives of regional associations, social partners and platforms of civil society at a public hearing convened on 25 November 2004,

- having regard to Rule 45 of its Rules of Procedure,

–   having regard to the report of the Committee on Constitutional Affairs and the opinions of the Committee on Foreign Affairs, the Committee on Development, the Committee on International Trade, the Committee on Budgets, the Committee on Budgetary Control, the Committee on Employment and Social Affairs, the Committee on the Environment, Public Health and Food Safety, the Committee on Industry, Research and Energy, the Committee on Regional Development, the Committee on Agriculture, the Committee on Fisheries, the Committee on Legal Affairs, the Committee on Civil Liberties, Justice and Home Affairs and the Committee on Petitions (A6-0070/2004),

Whereas:

A.   the European Union has, in the course of its history, played a substantial role in creating a continuously expanding area of peace and prosperity, democracy and freedom, justice and security,

B.   the Constitution consolidates these achievements and brings about innovations which are essential to maintaining and enhancing the capacity of the Union of twenty-five and potentially more Member States to act effectively internally and externally,

C.   the efforts to achieve a Constitution deployed by the European Parliament since its first direct election, have been crowned by the success of the Convention, which prepared the draft using a democratic, representative and transparent method that has fully proved its effectiveness, and which took account of the contributions of the citizens of Europe, resulting in a consensus which was left essentially unchanged by the Intergovernmental Conference,

D.   the Constitution, as a compromise that had to be acceptable to all Member States, inevitably left out some proposals, notably of the European Parliament and of the Convention, that would have, in the view of their authors, brought further improvements to the Union, many of which remain possible in the future,

E.   the agreement to the Constitution of every single national government in the European Union demonstrates that the elected governments of Member States all consider that this compromise is the basis on which they wish to work together in the future, and will require each of them to demonstrate maximum political commitment to ensuring ratification by 1 November 2006,

F.   the Constitution has been the object of some criticism voiced in public debate that does not reflect the real content and legal consequences of its provisions, insofar as the Constitution will not lead to the creation of a centralised superstate, will strengthen rather than weaken the Union's social dimension and does not ignore the historical and spiritual roots of Europe since it refers to its cultural, religious and humanist inheritance,

1.   Concludes that, taken as a whole, the Constitution is a good compromise and a vast improvement on the existing treaties, which will, once implemented, bring about visible benefits for citizens (and the European Parliament and the national parliaments as their democratic representation), the Member States (including their regions and local authorities) and the effective functioning of the European Union institutions, and thus for the Union as a whole;

Greater clarity as to the Union's nature and objectives

2.   Welcomes the fact that the Constitution provides citizens with more clarity as to the Union's nature and objectives and as to the relations between the Union and the Member States, notably because:

(a)   the complex set of European treaties is replaced by a single more readable document spelling out the objectives of the Union, its powers and their limits, its policy instruments and its institutions;

(b)   the Union's dual legitimacy is reaffirmed, and it is clarified that it is a Union of States and citizens;

(c)   the canon of values common to all the Member States, on which the Union is founded and which creates a strong bond between the Union's citizens, is made explicit and widened;

(d) the objectives of the Union as well as the principles governing its action and its relations with Member States are clarified and better defined;

(e) economic, social and territorial cohesion is reaffirmed as an objective of the Union;

(f) there are new provisions of general application concerning a high level of employment, the promotion of equality between women and men, the elimination of all kinds of discriminations, the fight against social exclusion and the promotion of social justice, social protection, a high level of education, training and health, the protection of the consumer, the promotion of sustainable development and the respect of services of general interest;

(g) the confusion between the «European Community» and «European Union» will end as the European Union becomes one single legal entity and structure;

(h) European legal acts are simplified and their terminology is clarified, using more understandable vocabulary: "European laws" and "European framework laws" replace the existing multiple types of act (regulations, directives, decisions, framework decisions, etc);

(i) it provides guarantees that the Union will never be a centralised all-powerful "superstate":

– the strong emphasis on decentralisation inherent in "united in diversity",

– the obligation to "respect the national identities of Member States, inherent in their fundamental structures, political and constitutional, inclusive of regional and local self-government",

> – the principles of conferred powers (whereby the Union's only competences are those conferred on it by the Member States), subsidiarity and proportionality,

> – the participation of the Member States themselves in the Union's decision-making system and in agreeing any changes to it;

(j) the inclusion of the symbols of the Union in the Constitution will improve awareness of the Union's institutions and their action;

(k) a solidarity clause between Member States provides citizens with an expectation of receiving support from all parts of the Union in case of a terrorist attack or a natural or man-made disaster;

Greater effectiveness and a strengthened role in the world

3. Welcomes the fact that, with the entry into force of the Constitution, the Union's institutions will be able to carry out their tasks more effectively, notably because:

(a) there is a significant increase in the areas in which the governments meeting in Council will decide by qualified majority voting rather than by unanimity, a vital factor if the Union of twenty-five Member States is to be able to function without being blocked by vetoes;

(b) the European Council will have a two-and-a-half-year chair instead of a six-month rotating one;

(c) there will, as of 2014, be a reduction in the number of members of the Commission based on an equal rotation between Member States;

(d) there will be a significant enhancement of the Union's visibility and capacity as a global actor:

> – the European Union's Foreign policy High Representative and the Commissioner for External Relations - two posts

causing duplication and confusion - will be merged into a single European Union Minister for Foreign Affairs, who will be a Vice President of the Commission and will chair the Foreign Affairs Council and be able to speak for the Union on those subjects where the latter has a common position,

–   there will be a single external action service which must be connected as closely as possible with the Commission and result in the strengthening of Europe as a community,

–   the conferral of legal personality, previously enjoyed by the European Community, on the Union will enhance its capacity to act in international relations and to be a party to international agreements,

–   the Union's capacity to develop common structures in the field of security and defence policy will be reinforced, while ensuring the necessary flexibility to cater for differing approaches of Member States to such matters;

(e)   the number of the Union's legislative instruments and the procedures for their adoption will be reduced; the distinction between legislative and executive instruments will be clarified;

(f)   action in the area of justice and home affairs will be subject to more effective procedures, promising tangible progress with regard to justice, security and immigration issues;

(g)   for a number of other matters, it will become easier to apply the successful Community method as soon as there is the political will to do so;

(h)   there is more room for flexible arrangements when not all Member States are willing or able to go ahead with certain policies at the same time;

More democratic accountability

4. Welcomes the fact that citizens will have greater control over the European Union's action by increased democratic accountability, notably due to the following improvements:

    (a) the adoption of all European Union legislation will be subject to the prior scrutiny of national parliaments and, with a few exceptions, the dual approval of both national governments (in the Council) and the directly elected European Parliament - a level of parliamentary scrutiny that exists in no other supranational or international structure;

    (b) national parliaments will receive all European Union proposals in good time to discuss them with their ministers before the Council adopts a position and will also gain the right to object to draft legislation if they feel it goes beyond the European Union's remit;

    (c) the European Parliament will as a rule decide on an equal footing with the Council on the Union's legislation;

    (d) the President of the Commission will be elected by the European Parliament, thereby establishing a link to the results of European elections;

    (e) the Union Minister for Foreign Affairs, appointed by the European Council in agreement with the Commission's President, will be accountable both to the European Parliament and to the European Council;

    (f) a new budgetary procedure will require the approval of both the Council and the European Parliament for all European Union expenditure, without exception, thus bringing all expenditure under full democratic control;

    (g) the exercise of delegated legislative powers by the Commission will be brought under a new system of supervision by the

European Parliament and the Council, enabling each of them to call back Commission decisions to which they object;

(h)   agencies, notably Europol, will be subject to greater parliamentary scrutiny;

(i)   the Council will meet in public when debating and adopting Union legislation;

(j)   the role of the Committee of the Regions is reinforced;

(k)   with regard to future revisions of the Constitution, the European Parliament, too, will have the power to submit proposals, and the scrutiny of any proposed revision must be carried out by a Convention unless Parliament agrees that this is not necessary;

More rights for citizens

5.   Welcomes the fact that the rights of citizens will be strengthened as a result of the following improvements:

(a)   the incorporation of the EU Charter of Fundamental Rights in Part II of the Constitution, which means that all provisions of European Union law and all action taken by the EU institutions or based on EU law will have to comply with those standards;

(b)   the Union is to accede to the European Convention on Human Rights, thereby making the Union subject to the same external review as its Member States;

(c)   new provisions will facilitate participation by citizens, the social partners, representative associations and civil society in the deliberations of the Union;

(d)   the introduction of a European citizens' initiative, which will enable citizens to submit proposals on matters where they consider that a legal act of the Union is required in order to implement the Constitution;

(e)   individuals will have greater access to justice in connection with European Union law;

Conclusions

6.   Endorses the Constitutional Treaty and wholeheartedly supports its ratification;

7.   Believes that this Constitution will provide a stable and lasting framework for the future development of the European Union that will allow for further enlargement while providing mechanisms for its revision when needed;

8.   Announces its intention of using the new right of initiative conferred upon it by the Constitution to propose improvements to the Constitution;

9.   Hopes that all Member States of the European Union will be in a position to achieve ratification by mid-2006;

10.   Reiterates its request that all possible efforts be deployed in order to inform European citizens clearly and objectively about the content of the Constitution; therefore invites the European institutions and the Member States, when distributing the text of the constitutional Treaty to citizens (in unabridged or summary versions), to make a clear distinction between the elements already in force in the existing treaties and new provisions introduced by the Constitution, with a view to educating the public and informing the debate; invites them also to recognise the role of civil society organisations within the ratification debates and to make available sufficient support to enable such organisations to engage their constituencies in these debates across the EU in order to promote the active involvement of citizens in the discussions on ratification;

o

o   o

11.   Instructs its President to forward this resolution and the report of the Committee on Constitutional Affairs to the national parliaments of the Member States, the Council, the Commission and the former Members of the European Convention, and to ensure that Parliament's services, including its Information Offices, provide ample information about the Constitution and Parliament's position on it.

---

[1]   OJ C 364, 18.12.2000, p.1.

[2]   Laeken European Council, Laeken declaration on the future of the Union, SN 273/01, 15.12.2001.

[3]   Resolution of 14.2.1984 on the draft Treaty establishing the European Union (OJ C 77, 19.3.1984, p. 5, rapporteur: Altiero Spinelli, 1-1200/1983).
Resolution of 11.7.1990 on the European Parliament's guidelines for a draft constitution for the European Union (OJ C 231, 17.9.1990, p. 91, rapporteur: Emilio Colombo, A3-0165/1990).
Resolution of 12.12.1990 on the constitutional basis of European Union (OJ C 19, 28.1.1991, p. 65, rapporteur: Emilio Colombo, A3-0301/1990).
Resolution of 10.2.1994 on the Constitution of the European Union (OJ C 61, 28.2.1994, p. 155, rapporteur: Fernand Herman, A3-0064/1994).
Resolution of 25.10.2000 on the constitutionalisation of the Treaties (OJ C 197, 12.7.2001, p. 186, rapporteur: Olivier Duhamel, A5-0289/2000).

[4]   Resolution of 14.3.1990 on the Intergovernmental Conference in the context of Parliament's strategy for European Union (OJ C 96, 17.4.1990, p. 114, rapporteur: David Martin, A3-0047/1990).
Resolution of 11.7.1990 on the Intergovernmental Conference in the context of Parliament's strategy for European Union (OJ C 231, 17.9.1990, p. 97, rapporteur: David Martin, A3-0166/1990).
Resolution of 22.11.1990 on the Intergovernmental Conferences in the context of Parliament's strategy for European Union (OJ C 324, 24.12.1990, p. 219, rapporteur: David Martin, A3-0270/1990).
Resolution of 22.11.1990 embodying Parliament's opinion on the convening of the Intergovernmental Conferences on Economic and Monetary Union and on Political Union (OJ C 324, 24.12.1990, p. 238, rapporteur: David Martin, A3-0281/1990).
Resolution of 17.5.1995 on the functioning of the Treaty on European Union with a view to the 1996 Intergovernmental Conference - Implementation and development of the Union (OJ C 151, 19.6.1995, p. 56. rapporteurs: Jean-Louis Bourlanges and David Martin, A4-0102/1995).
Resolution of 13.3.1996 embodying (i) Parliament's opinion on the convening of the Intergovernmental Conference, and (ii) an evaluation of the work of the Reflection Group and a definition of the political priorities of the European Parliament with a view to the Intergovernmental Conference (OJ C 96, 1.4.1996, p. 77, rapporteurs : Raymonde Dury and Hanja Maij-Weggen, A4-0068/1996).
Resolution of 18.11.1999 on the preparation of the reform of the Treaties and the next Intergovernmental Conference (OJ C 189, 7.7.2000, p. 222, rapporteurs: Giorgos Dimitrakopoulos and Jo Leinen, A5-0058/1999).
Resolution of 3.2.2000 on the convening of the Intergovernmental Conference (OJ C 309, 27.10.2000, p. 85, rapporteurs: Giorgos Dimitrakopoulos and Jo Leinen, A5-0018/2000).
Resolution of 16.3.2000 on the drafting of a European Union Charter of Fundamental Rights (OJ C 377, 29.12.2000, p. 329, rapporteurs: Andrew Duff and Johannes Voggenhuber, A5-0064/2000).
Resolution of 13.4.2000 containing the European Parliament's proposals for the Intergovernmental Conference (OJ C 40, 7.2.2001, p. 409, rapporteurs: Giorgos Dimitrakopoulos and Jo Leinen, A5-0086/2000).

[5]   Resolution of 16.1.1986 on the position of the European Parliament on the Single Act approved by the Intergovernmental Conference on 16 and 17 December 1985 (OJ C 36, 17.2.1986, p. 144, rapporteur: Altiero Spinelli, A2-0199/1985).

Resolution of 11.12.1986 on the Single European Act (OJ C 7, 12.1.1987, p. 105, rapporteur: Luis Planas Puchades, A2-0169/1986).
Resolution of 7.4.1992 on the results of the Intergovernmental Conferences (OJ C 125, 18.5.1992, p. 81, rapporteurs: David Martin and Fernand Herman, A3-0123/1992).
Resolution of 19.11.1997 on the Amsterdam Treaty (OJ C 371, 8.12.1997, p. 99, rapporteurs: Iñigo Méndez de Vigo and Dimitris Tsatsos, A4-0347/1997).
Resolution of 31.5.2001 on the Treaty of Nice and the future of the European Union (OJ C 47 E, 21.2.2002, p. 108, rapporteurs: Iñigo Méndez de Vigo and António José Seguro, A5-0168/2001).

[6]   Resolution of 29.11.2001 on the constitutional process and the future of the Union (OJ C 153 E, 27.6.2002, p. 310, rapporteurs: Jo Leinen and Iñigo Méndez de Vigo, A5-0368/2001).
Resolution of 24.9.2003 on the draft Treaty establishing a Constitution for Europe and the European Parliament's opinion on the convening of the Intergovernmental Conference (OJ C 77 E, 26.3.2004, p. 255, rapporteurs: José María Gil-Robles Gil-Delgado and Dimitris Tsatsos, A5-0299/2003).

[7]   CdR 354/2003 fin, not yet published in the Official Journal.

[8]   CESE 1416/2004, not yet published in the Official Journal.

[9]   Items 8.2 and 8.3, P6_PV(2004)09-14.

TREATY ESTABLISHING A CONSTITUTION FOR EUROPE

TABLE OF CONTENTS

PART II: THE CHARTER OF FUNDAMENTAL RIGHTS OF THE UNION

PREAMBLE

TITLE I –   DIGNITY

TITLE II –   FREEDOMS

TITLE III –   EQUALITY

TITLE IV –   SOLIDARITY

TITLE V –   CITIZENS' RIGHTS

TITLE VI –   JUSTICE

TITLE VII –   GENERAL PROVISIONS GOVERNING THE INTERPRETATION AND
               APPLICATION OF THE CHARTER

PART III: THE POLICIES AND FUNCTIONING OF THE UNION

TITLE I –   PROVISIONS OF GENERAL APPLICATION

TITLE II –   NON-DISCRIMINATION AND CITIZENSHIP

TITLE III –   INTERNAL POLICIES AND ACTION

CHAPTER I – INTERNAL MARKET
Section 1 – Establishment and functioning of the Internal Market
Section 2 – Free movement of persons and services
Subsection 1 – Workers
Subsection 2 – Freedom of establishment
Subsection 3 – Freedom to provide services
Section 3 – Free movement of goods
Subsection 1 – Customs Union
Subsection 2 – Customs cooperation
Subsection 3 – Prohibition of quantitative restrictions
Section 4 – Capital and payments
Section 5 – Rules on competition
Subsection 1 – Rules applying to undertakings
Subsection 2 – Aids granted by Member States
Section 6 – Fiscal provisions
Section 7 – Common provisions

CHAPTER II – ECONOMIC AND MONETARY POLICY
Section 1 – Economic policy

PREAMBLE

HIS MAJESTY THE KING OF THE BELGIANS, THE PRESIDENT OF THE CZECH REPUBLIC, HER MAJESTY THE QUEEN OF DENMARK, THE PRESIDENT OF THE FEDERAL REPUBLIC OF GERMANY, THE PRESIDENT OF THE REPUBLIC OF ESTONIA, THE PRESIDENT OF THE HELLENIC REPUBLIC, HIS MAJESTY THE KING OF SPAIN, THE PRESIDENT OF THE FRENCH REPUBLIC, THE PRESIDENT OF IRELAND, THE PRESIDENT OF THE ITALIAN REPUBLIC, THE PRESIDENT OF THE REPUBLIC OF CYPRUS, THE PRESIDENT OF THE REPUBLIC OF LATVIA, THE PRESIDENT OF THE REPUBLIC OF LITHUANIA, HIS ROYAL HIGHNESS THE GRAND DUKE OF LUXEMBOURG, THE PRESIDENT OF THE REPUBLIC OF HUNGARY, THE PRESIDENT OF MALTA, HER MAJESTY THE QUEEN OF THE NETHERLANDS, THE FEDERAL PRESIDENT OF THE REPUBLIC OF AUSTRIA, THE PRESIDENT OF THE REPUBLIC OF POLAND, THE PRESIDENT OF THE PORTUGUESE REPUBLIC, THE PRESIDENT OF THE REPUBLIC OF SLOVENIA, THE PRESIDENT OF THE SLOVAK REPUBLIC, THE PRESIDENT OF THE REPUBLIC OF FINLAND, THE GOVERNMENT OF THE KINGDOM OF SWEDEN, HER MAJESTY THE QUEEN OF THE UNITED KINGDOM OF GREAT BRITAIN AND NORTHERN IRELAND,

DRAWING INSPIRATION from the cultural, religious and humanist inheritance of Europe, from which have developed the universal values of the inviolable and inalienable rights of the human person, freedom, democracy, equality and the rule of law,

BELIEVING that Europe, reunited after bitter experiences, intends to continue along the path of civilisation, progress and prosperity, for the good of all its inhabitants, including the weakest and most deprived; that it wishes to remain a continent open to culture, learning and social progress; and that it wishes to deepen the democratic and transparent nature of its public life, and to strive for peace, justice and solidarity throughout the world,

CONVINCED that, while remaining proud of their own national identities and history, the peoples of Europe are determined to transcend their former divisions and, united ever more closely, to forge a common destiny,

CONVINCED that, thus "United in diversity", Europe offers them the best chance of pursuing, with due regard for the rights of each individual and in awareness of their responsibilities towards future generations and the Earth, the great venture which makes of it a special area of human hope,

DETERMINED to continue the work accomplished within the framework of the Treaties establishing the European Communities and the Treaty on European Union, by ensuring the continuity of the Community *acquis*,

GRATEFUL to the members of the European Convention for having prepared the draft of this Constitution on behalf of the citizens and States of Europe,

HAVE DESIGNATED AS THEIR PLENIPOTENTIARIES:

HIS MAJESTY THE KING OF THE BELGIANS,

Guy VERHOFSTADT
Prime Minister

Karel DE GUCHT
Minister for Foreign Affairs

THE PRESIDENT OF THE CZECH REPUBLIC,

Stanislav GROSS
Prime Minister

Cyril SVOBODA
Minister for Foreign Affairs

HER MAJESTY THE QUEEN OF DENMARK,

Anders Fogh RASMUSSEN
Prime Minister

Per Stig MØLLER
Minister for Foreign Affairs

THE PRESIDENT OF THE FEDERAL REPUBLIC OF GERMANY,

Gerhard SCHRÖDER
Federal Chancellor

Joseph FISCHER
Federal Minister for Foreign Affairs and Deputy Federal Chancellor

THE PRESIDENT OF THE REPUBLIC OF ESTONIA,

Juhan PARTS
Prime Minister

Kristiina OJULAND
Minister for Foreign Affairs

THE PRESIDENT OF THE HELLENIC REPUBLIC,

Kostas KARAMANLIS
Prime Minister

Petros G. MOLYVIATIS
Minister of Foreign Affairs

HIS MAJESTY THE KING OF SPAIN,

José Luis RODRÍGUEZ ZAPATERO
President of the Government

Miguel Angel MORATINOS CUYAUBÉ
Minister for External Affairs and Cooperation

THE PRESIDENT OF THE FRENCH REPUBLIC,

Jacques CHIRAC
President

Jean-Pierre RAFFARIN
Prime Minister

Michel BARNIER
Minister for Foreign Affairs

THE PRESIDENT OF IRELAND,

Bertie AHERN
Taoiseach

Dermot AHERN
Minister for Foreign Affairs

THE PRESIDENT OF THE ITALIAN REPUBLIC,

Silvio BERLUSCONI
Prime Minister

Franco FRATTINI
Minister for Foreign Affairs

THE PRESIDENT OF THE REPUBLIC OF CYPRUS,

Tassos PAPADOPOULOS
President

George IACOVOU
Minister for Foreign Affairs

THE PRESIDENT OF THE REPUBLIC OF LATVIA,

Vaira VĪĶE FREIBERGA
President

Indulis EMSIS
Prime Minister

Artis PABRIKS
Minister for Foreign Affairs

THE PRESIDENT OF THE REPUBLIC OF LITHUANIA,

Valdas ADAMKUS
President

Algirdas Mykolas BRAZAUSKAS
Prime Minister

Antanas VALIONIS
Minister of Foreign Affairs

HIS ROYAL HIGHNESS THE GRAND DUKE OF LUXEMBOURG,

Jean-Claude JUNCKER
Prime Minister, Ministre d'Etat

Jean ASSELBORN
Deputy Prime Minister, Minister for Foreign Affairs and Immigration

THE PRESIDENT OF THE REPUBLIC OF HUNGARY,

Ferenc GYURCSÁNY
Prime Minister

László KOVÁCS
Minister for Foreign Affairs

THE PRESIDENT OF MALTA,

The Hon Lawrence GONZI
Prime Minister

The Hon Michael FRENDO
Minister for Foreign Affairs

HER MAJESTY THE QUEEN OF THE NETHERLANDS,

Dr. J. P. BALKENENDE
Prime Minister

Dr. B. R. BOT
Minister for Foreign Affairs

THE FEDERAL PRESIDENT OF THE REPUBLIC OF AUSTRIA,

Dr. Wolfgang SCHÜSSEL
Federal Chancellor

Dr. Ursula PLASSNIK
Federal Minister for Foreign Affairs

THE PRESIDENT OF THE REPUBLIC OF POLAND,

Marek BELKA
Prime Minister

Włodzimierz CIMOSZEWICZ
Minister for Foreign Affairs

THE PRESIDENT OF THE PORTUGUESE REPUBLIC,

Pedro Miguel DE SANTANA LOPES
Prime Minister

António Victor MARTINS MONTEIRO
Minister for Foreign Affairs and the Portuguese Communities

THE PRESIDENT OF THE REPUBLIC OF SLOVENIA,

Anton ROP
President of the Government

Ivo VAJGL
Minister for Foreign Affairs

THE PRESIDENT OF THE SLOVAK REPUBLIC,

Mikuláš DZURINDA
Prime Minister

Eduard KUKAN
Minister for Foreign Affairs

THE PRESIDENT OF THE REPUBLIC OF FINLAND,

Matti VANHANEN
Prime Minister

Erkki TUOMIOJA
Minister for Foreign Affairs

THE GOVERNMENT OF THE KINGDOM OF SWEDEN

Göran PERSSON
Prime Minister

Laila FREIVALDS
Minister for Foreign Affairs

HER MAJESTY THE QUEEN OF THE UNITED KINGDOM OF GREAT BRITAIN AND NORTHERN IRELAND,

The Rt. Hon Tony BLAIR
Prime Minister

The Rt. Hon Jack STRAW
Secretary of State for Foreign and Commonwealth Affairs

WHO, having exchanged their full powers, found in good and due form, have agreed as follows:

PART I

TITLE I

DEFINITION AND OBJECTIVES OF THE UNION

ARTICLE I-1

Establishment of the Union

1.   Reflecting the will of the citizens and States of Europe to build a common future, this Constitution establishes the European Union, on which the Member States confer competences to attain objectives they have in common. The Union shall coordinate the policies by which the Member States aim to achieve these objectives, and shall exercise on a Community basis the competences they confer on it.

2.   The Union shall be open to all European States which respect its values and are committed to promoting them together.

ARTICLE I-2

The Union's values

The Union is founded on the values of respect for human dignity, freedom, democracy, equality, the rule of law and respect for human rights, including the rights of persons belonging to minorities. These values are common to the Member States in a society in which pluralism, non-discrimination, tolerance, justice, solidarity and equality between women and men prevail.

ARTICLE I-3

The Union's objectives

1.   The Union's aim is to promote peace, its values and the well-being of its peoples.

2.   The Union shall offer its citizens an area of freedom, security and justice without internal frontiers, and an internal market where competition is free and undistorted.

3.   The Union shall work for the sustainable development of Europe based on balanced economic growth and price stability, a highly competitive social market economy, aiming at full employment and social progress, and a high level of protection and improvement of the quality of the environment. It shall promote scientific and technological advance.

It shall combat social exclusion and discrimination, and shall promote social justice and protection, equality between women and men, solidarity between generations and protection of the rights of the child.

It shall promote economic, social and territorial cohesion, and solidarity among Member States.

It shall respect its rich cultural and linguistic diversity, and shall ensure that Europe's cultural heritage is safeguarded and enhanced.

4.   In its relations with the wider world, the Union shall uphold and promote its values and interests. It shall contribute to peace, security, the sustainable development of the Earth, solidarity and mutual respect among peoples, free and fair trade, eradication of poverty and the protection of human rights, in particular the rights of the child, as well as to the strict observance and the development of international law, including respect for the principles of the United Nations Charter.

5.   The Union shall pursue its objectives by appropriate means commensurate with the competences which are conferred upon it in the Constitution.

ARTICLE I-4

Fundamental freedoms and non-discrimination

1.   The free movement of persons, services, goods and capital, and freedom of establishment shall be guaranteed within and by the Union, in accordance with the Constitution.

2.   Within the scope of the Constitution, and without prejudice to any of its specific provisions, any discrimination on grounds of nationality shall be prohibited.

ARTICLE I-5

Relations between the Union and the Member States

1.   The Union shall respect the equality of Member States before the Constitution as well as their national identities, inherent in their fundamental structures, political and constitutional, inclusive of regional and local self-government. It shall respect their essential State functions, including ensuring the territorial integrity of the State, maintaining law and order and safeguarding national security.

2.   Pursuant to the principle of sincere cooperation, the Union and the Member States shall, in full mutual respect, assist each other in carrying out tasks which flow from the Constitution.

The Member States shall take any appropriate measure, general or particular, to ensure fulfilment of the obligations arising out of the Constitution or resulting from the acts of the institutions of the Union.

The Member States shall facilitate the achievement of the Union's tasks and refrain from any measure which could jeopardise the attainment of the Union's objectives.

ARTICLE I-6

Union law

The Constitution and law adopted by the institutions of the Union in exercising competences conferred on it shall have primacy over the law of the Member States.

ARTICLE I-7

Legal personality

The Union shall have legal personality.

ARTICLE I-8

The symbols of the Union

The flag of the Union shall be a circle of twelve golden stars on a blue background.

The anthem of the Union shall be based on the "Ode to Joy" from the Ninth Symphony by Ludwig van Beethoven.

The motto of the Union shall be: "United in diversity".

The currency of the Union shall be the euro.

Europe day shall be celebrated on 9 May throughout the Union.

TITLE II

FUNDAMENTAL RIGHTS AND CITIZENSHIP OF THE UNION

ARTICLE I-9

Fundamental rights

1.   The Union shall recognise the rights, freedoms and principles set out in the Charter of Fundamental Rights which constitutes Part II.

2.   The Union shall accede to the European Convention for the Protection of Human Rights and Fundamental Freedoms. Such accession shall not affect the Union's competences as defined in the Constitution.

3.   Fundamental rights, as guaranteed by the European Convention for the Protection of Human Rights and Fundamental Freedoms and as they result from the constitutional traditions common to the Member States, shall constitute general principles of the Union's law.

ARTICLE I-10

Citizenship of the Union

1.   Every national of a Member State shall be a citizen of the Union. Citizenship of the Union shall be additional to national citizenship and shall not replace it.

2.   Citizens of the Union shall enjoy the rights and be subject to the duties provided for in the Constitution. They shall have:

(a)   the right to move and reside freely within the territory of the Member States;

(b)   the right to vote and to stand as candidates in elections to the European Parliament and in municipal elections in their Member State of residence, under the same conditions as nationals of that State;

(c)   the right to enjoy, in the territory of a third country in which the Member State of which they are nationals is not represented, the protection of the diplomatic and consular authorities of any Member State on the same conditions as the nationals of that State;

(d)   the right to petition the European Parliament, to apply to the European Ombudsman, and to address the institutions and advisory bodies of the Union in any of the Constitution's languages and to obtain a reply in the same language.

These rights shall be exercised in accordance with the conditions and limits defined by the Constitution and by the measures adopted thereunder.

TITLE III

UNION COMPETENCES

ARTICLE I-11

Fundamental principles

1.   The limits of Union competences are governed by the principle of conferral. The use of Union competences is governed by the principles of subsidiarity and proportionality.

2.   Under the principle of conferral, the Union shall act within the limits of the competences conferred upon it by the Member States in the Constitution to attain the objectives set out in the Constitution. Competences not conferred upon the Union in the Constitution remain with the Member States.

3.   Under the principle of subsidiarity, in areas which do not fall within its exclusive competence, the Union shall act only if and insofar as the objectives of the proposed action cannot be sufficiently achieved by the Member States, either at central level or at regional and local level, but can rather, by reason of the scale or effects of the proposed action, be better achieved at Union level.

The institutions of the Union shall apply the principle of subsidiarity as laid down in the Protocol on the application of the principles of subsidiarity and proportionality. National Parliaments shall ensure compliance with that principle in accordance with the procedure set out in that Protocol.

4.   Under the principle of proportionality, the content and form of Union action shall not exceed what is necessary to achieve the objectives of the Constitution.

The institutions of the Union shall apply the principle of proportionality as laid down in the Protocol on the application of the principles of subsidiarity and proportionality.

ARTICLE I-12

Categories of competence

1.   When the Constitution confers on the Union exclusive competence in a specific area, only the Union may legislate and adopt legally binding acts, the Member States being able to do so themselves only if so empowered by the Union or for the implementation of Union acts.

2.   When the Constitution confers on the Union a competence shared with the Member States in a specific area, the Union and the Member States may legislate and adopt legally binding acts in that area. The Member States shall exercise their competence to the extent that the Union has not exercised, or has decided to cease exercising, its competence.

3.   The Member States shall coordinate their economic and employment policies within arrangements as determined by Part III, which the Union shall have competence to provide.

4.   The Union shall have competence to define and implement a common foreign and security policy, including the progressive framing of a common defence policy.

5.   In certain areas and under the conditions laid down in the Constitution, the Union shall have competence to carry out actions to support, coordinate or supplement the actions of the Member States, without thereby superseding their competence in these areas.

Legally binding acts of the Union adopted on the basis of the provisions in Part III relating to these areas shall not entail harmonisation of Member States' laws or regulations.

6.   The scope of and arrangements for exercising the Union's competences shall be determined by the provisions relating to each area in Part III.

ARTICLE I-13

Areas of exclusive competence

1.   The Union shall have exclusive competence in the following areas:

(a)   customs union;

(b)   the establishing of the competition rules necessary for the functioning of the internal market;

(c)   monetary policy for the Member States whose currency is the euro;

(d)   the conservation of marine biological resources under the common fisheries policy;

(e)   common commercial policy.

2.   The Union shall also have exclusive competence for the conclusion of an international agreement when its conclusion is provided for in a legislative act of the Union or is necessary to enable the Union to exercise its internal competence, or insofar as its conclusion may affect common rules or alter their scope.

ARTICLE I-14

Areas of shared competence

1.   The Union shall share competence with the Member States where the Constitution confers on it a competence which does not relate to the areas referred to in Articles I-13 and I-17.

2.   Shared competence between the Union and the Member States applies in the following principal areas:

(a)   internal market;

(b)   social policy, for the aspects defined in Part III;

(c)   economic, social and territorial cohesion;

(d)   agriculture and fisheries, excluding the conservation of marine biological resources;

(e)   environment;

(f)   consumer protection;

(g)   transport;

(h)   trans-European networks;

(i)   energy;

(j)   area of freedom, security and justice;

(k)   common safety concerns in public health matters, for the aspects defined in Part III.

3.   In the areas of research, technological development and space, the Union shall have competence to carry out activities, in particular to define and implement programmes; however, the exercise of that competence shall not result in Member States being prevented from exercising theirs.

4.   In the areas of development cooperation and humanitarian aid, the Union shall have competence to carry out activities and conduct a common policy; however, the exercise of that competence shall not result in Member States being prevented from exercising theirs.

ARTICLE I-15

The coordination of economic and employment policies

1.   The Member States shall coordinate their economic policies within the Union. To this end, the Council of Ministers shall adopt measures, in particular broad guidelines for these policies.

Specific provisions shall apply to those Member States whose currency is the euro.

2.   The Union shall take measures to ensure coordination of the employment policies of the Member States, in particular by defining guidelines for these policies.

3.   The Union may take initiatives to ensure coordination of Member States' social policies.

ARTICLE I-16

The common foreign and security policy

1.   The Union's competence in matters of common foreign and security policy shall cover all areas of foreign policy and all questions relating to the Union's security, including the progressive framing of a common defence policy that might lead to a common defence.

2.   Member States shall actively and unreservedly support the Union's common foreign and security policy in a spirit of loyalty and mutual solidarity and shall comply with the Union's action in this area. They shall refrain from action contrary to the Union's interests or likely to impair its effectiveness.

ARTICLE I-17

Areas of supporting, coordinating or complementary action

The Union shall have competence to carry out supporting, coordinating or complementary action. The areas of such action shall, at European level, be:

(a)   protection and improvement of human health;

(b)   industry;

(c)   culture;

(d)   tourism;

(e)   education, youth, sport and vocational training;

(f)   civil protection;

(g)   administrative cooperation.

ARTICLE I-18

Flexibility clause

1.   If action by the Union should prove necessary, within the framework of the policies defined in Part III, to attain one of the objectives set out in the Constitution, and the Constitution has not provided the necessary powers, the Council of Ministers, acting unanimously on a proposal from the European Commission and after obtaining the consent of the European Parliament, shall adopt the appropriate measures.

2.   Using the procedure for monitoring the subsidiarity principle referred to in Article I-11(3), the European Commission shall draw national Parliaments' attention to proposals based on this Article.

3.   Measures based on this Article shall not entail harmonisation of Member States' laws or regulations in cases where the Constitution excludes such harmonisation.

TITLE IV

THE UNION'S INSTITUTIONS AND BODIES

CHAPTER I
THE INSTITUTIONAL FRAMEWORK

ARTICLE I-19

The Union's institutions

1.   The Union shall have an institutional framework which shall aim to:

–   promote its values,

–   advance its objectives,

–   serve its interests, those of its citizens and those of the Member States,

–   ensure the consistency, effectiveness and continuity of its policies and actions.

This institutional framework comprises:

–   The European Parliament,

–   The European Council,

–   The Council of Ministers (hereinafter referred to as the "Council"),

–   The European Commission (hereinafter referred to as the "Commission"),

–   The Court of Justice of the European Union.

2.   Each institution shall act within the limits of the powers conferred on it in the Constitution, and in conformity with the procedures and conditions set out in it. The institutions shall practise mutual sincere cooperation.

ARTICLE I-20

The European Parliament

1.   The European Parliament shall, jointly with the Council, exercise legislative and budgetary functions. It shall exercise functions of political control and consultation as laid down in the Constitution. It shall elect the President of the Commission.

2.   The European Parliament shall be composed of representatives of the Union's citizens. They shall not exceed seven hundred and fifty in number. Representation of citizens shall

be degressively proportional, with a minimum threshold of six members per Member State. No Member State shall be allocated more than ninety-six seats.

The European Council shall adopt by unanimity, on the initiative of the European Parliament and with its consent, a European decision establishing the composition of the European Parliament, respecting the principles referred to in the first subparagraph.

3.   The members of the European Parliament shall be elected for a term of five years by direct universal suffrage in a free and secret ballot.

4.   The European Parliament shall elect its President and its officers from among its members.

ARTICLE I-21

The European Council

1.   The European Council shall provide the Union with the necessary impetus for its development and shall define the general political directions and priorities thereof. It shall not exercise legislative functions.

2.   The European Council shall consist of the Heads of State or Government of the Member States, together with its President and the President of the Commission. The Union Minister for Foreign Affairs shall take part in its work.

3.   The European Council shall meet quarterly, convened by its President. When the agenda so requires, the members of the European Council may decide each to be assisted by a minister and, in the case of the President of the Commission, by a member of the Commission. When the situation so requires, the President shall convene a special meeting of the European Council.

4.   Except where the Constitution provides otherwise, decisions of the European Council shall be taken by consensus.

ARTICLE I-22

The European Council President

1.   The European Council shall elect its President, by a qualified majority, for a term of two and a half years, renewable once. In the event of an impediment or serious misconduct, the European Council can end his or her term of office in accordance with the same procedure.

2.   The President of the European Council:

(a)   shall chair it and drive forward its work;

(b)   shall ensure the preparation and continuity of the work of the European Council in cooperation with the President of the Commission, and on the basis of the work of the General Affairs Council;

(c)   shall endeavour to facilitate cohesion and consensus within the European Council;

(d)   shall present a report to the European Parliament after each of the meetings of the European Council.

The President of the European Council shall, at his or her level and in that capacity, ensure the external representation of the Union on issues concerning its common foreign and security policy, without prejudice to the powers of the Union Minister for Foreign Affairs.

3.   The President of the European Council shall not hold a national office.

ARTICLE I-23

The Council of Ministers

1.   The Council shall, jointly with the European Parliament, exercise legislative and budgetary functions. It shall carry out policy-making and coordinating functions as laid down in the Constitution.

2.   The Council shall consist of a representative of each Member State at ministerial level, who may commit the government of the Member State in question and cast its vote.

3.   The Council shall act by a qualified majority except where the Constitution provides otherwise.

ARTICLE I-24

Configurations of the Council of Ministers

1.   The Council shall meet in different configurations.

2.   The General Affairs Council shall ensure consistency in the work of the different Council configurations.

It shall prepare and ensure the follow-up to meetings of the European Council, in liaison with the President of the European Council and the Commission.

3.   The Foreign Affairs Council shall elaborate the Union's external action on the basis of strategic guidelines laid down by the European Council and ensure that the Union's action is consistent.

4.   The European Council shall adopt by a qualified majority a European decision establishing the list of other Council configurations.

5.   A Committee of Permanent Representatives of the Governments of the Member States shall be responsible for preparing the work of the Council.

6.   The Council shall meet in public when it deliberates and votes on a draft legislative act. To this end, each Council meeting shall be divided into two parts, dealing respectively with deliberations on Union legislative acts and non-legislative activities.

7.   The Presidency of Council configurations, other than that of Foreign Affairs, shall be held by Member State representatives in the Council on the basis of equal rotation, in accordance

with the conditions established by a European decision of the European Council. The European Council shall act by a qualified majority.

ARTICLE I-25

Definition of qualified majority within the European Council and the Council

1.   A qualified majority shall be defined as at least 55% of the members of the Council, comprising at least fifteen of them and representing Member States comprising at least 65% of the population of the Union.

A blocking minority must include at least four Council members, failing which the qualified majority shall be deemed attained.

2.   By way of derogation from paragraph 1, when the Council does not act on a proposal from the Commission or from the Union Minister for Foreign Affairs, the qualified majority shall be defined as at least 72% of the members of the Council, representing Member States comprising at least 65% of the population of the Union.

3.   Paragraphs 1 and 2 shall apply to the European Council when it is acting by a qualified majority.

4.   Within the European Council, its President and the President of the Commission shall not take part in the vote.

ARTICLE I-26

The European Commission

1.   The Commission shall promote the general interest of the Union and take appropriate initiatives to that end. It shall ensure the application of the Constitution, and measures adopted by the institutions pursuant to the Constitution. It shall oversee the application of Union law under the control of the Court of Justice of the European Union. It shall execute the budget and manage programmes. It shall exercise coordinating, executive and management functions, as laid down in the Constitution. With the exception of the common foreign and security policy, and other cases provided for in the Constitution, it shall ensure the Union's external representation. It shall initiate the Union's annual and multiannual programming with a view to achieving interinstitutional agreements.

2.   Union legislative acts may be adopted only on the basis of a Commission proposal, except where the Constitution provides otherwise. Other acts shall be adopted on the basis of a Commission proposal where the Constitution so provides.

3.   The Commission's term of office shall be five years.

4.   The members of the Commission shall be chosen on the ground of their general competence and European commitment from persons whose independence is beyond doubt.

5.   The first Commission appointed under the provisions of the Constitution shall consist of one national of each Member State, including its President and the Union Minister for Foreign Affairs who shall be one of its Vice-Presidents.

6.   As from the end of the term of office of the Commission referred to in paragraph 5, the Commission shall consist of a number of members, including its President and the Union Minister for Foreign Affairs, corresponding to two thirds of the number of Member States, unless the European Council, acting unanimously, decides to alter this number.

The members of the Commission shall be selected from among the nationals of the Member States on the basis of a system of equal rotation between the Member States. This system shall be established by a European decision adopted unanimously by the European Council and on the basis of the following principles:

(a)   Member States shall be treated on a strictly equal footing as regards determination of the sequence of, and the time spent by, their nationals as members of the Commission; consequently, the difference between the total number of terms of office held by nationals of any given pair of Member States may never be more than one;

(b)   subject to point (a), each successive Commission shall be so composed as to reflect satisfactorily the demographic and geographical range of all the Member States.

7.   In carrying out its responsibilities, the Commission shall be completely independent. Without prejudice to Article I-28(2), the members of the Commission shall neither seek nor take instructions from any government or other institution, body, office or entity. They shall refrain from any action incompatible with their duties or the performance of their tasks.

8.   The Commission, as a body, shall be responsible to the European Parliament. In accordance with Article III-340, the European Parliament may vote on a censure motion on the Commission. If such a motion is carried, the members of the Commission shall resign as a body and the Union Minister for Foreign Affairs shall resign from the duties that he or she carries out in the Commission.

ARTICLE I-27

The President of the European Commission

1.   Taking into account the elections to the European Parliament and after having held the appropriate consultations, the European Council, acting by a qualified majority, shall propose to the European Parliament a candidate for President of the Commission. This candidate shall be elected by the European Parliament by a majority of its component members. If he or she does not obtain the required majority, the European Council, acting by a qualified majority, shall within one month propose a new candidate who shall be elected by the European Parliament following the same procedure.

2.   The Council, by common accord with the President-elect, shall adopt the list of the other persons whom it proposes for appointment as members of the Commission. They shall be selected, on the basis of the suggestions made by Member States, in accordance with the criteria set out in Article I-26(4) and (6), second subparagraph.

The President, the Union Minister for Foreign Affairs and the other members of the Commission shall be subject as a body to a vote of consent by the European Parliament. On the basis of this consent the Commission shall be appointed by the European Council, acting by a qualified majority.

3.   The President of the Commission shall:

(a)   lay down guidelines within which the Commission is to work;

(b)   decide on the internal organisation of the Commission, ensuring that it acts consistently, efficiently and as a collegiate body;

(c)   appoint Vice-Presidents, other than the Union Minister for Foreign Affairs, from among the members of the Commission.

A member of the Commission shall resign if the President so requests. The Union Minister for Foreign Affairs shall resign, in accordance with the procedure set out in Article I-28(1), if the President so requests.

ARTICLE I-28

The Union Minister for Foreign Affairs

1.   The European Council, acting by a qualified majority, with the agreement of the President of the Commission, shall appoint the Union Minister for Foreign Affairs. The European Council may end his or her term of office by the same procedure.

2.   The Union Minister for Foreign Affairs shall conduct the Union's common foreign and security policy. He or she shall contribute by his or her proposals to the development of that policy, which he or she shall carry out as mandated by the Council. The same shall apply to the common security and defence policy.

3.   The Union Minister for Foreign Affairs shall preside over the Foreign Affairs Council.

4.   The Union Minister for Foreign Affairs shall be one of the Vice-Presidents of the Commission. He or she shall ensure the consistency of the Union's external action. He or she shall be responsible within the Commission for responsibilities incumbent on it in external relations and for coordinating other aspects of the Union's external action. In exercising these responsibilities within the Commission, and only for these responsibilities, the Union Minister for Foreign Affairs shall be bound by Commission procedures to the extent that this is consistent with paragraphs 2 and 3.

ARTICLE I-29

The Court of Justice of the European Union

1.   The Court of Justice of the European Union shall include the Court of Justice, the General Court and specialised courts. It shall ensure that in the interpretation and application of the Constitution the law is observed.

Member States shall provide remedies sufficient to ensure effective legal protection in the fields covered by Union law.

2.   The Court of Justice shall consist of one judge from each Member State. It shall be assisted by Advocates-General.

The General Court shall include at least one judge per Member State.

The judges and the Advocates-General of the Court of Justice and the judges of the General Court shall be chosen from persons whose independence is beyond doubt and who satisfy the conditions set out in Articles III-355 and III-356. They shall be appointed by common accord of the governments of the Member States for six years. Retiring judges and Advocates-General may be reappointed.

3.   The Court of Justice of the European Union shall in accordance with Part III:

(a)   rule on actions brought by a Member State, an institution or a natural or legal person;

(b)   give preliminary rulings, at the request of courts or tribunals of the Member States, on the interpretation of Union law or the validity of acts adopted by the institutions;

(c)   rule in other cases provided for in the Constitution.

CHAPTER II

THE OTHER UNION INSTITUTIONS AND ADVISORY BODIES

ARTICLE I-30

The European Central Bank

1.   The European Central Bank, together with the national central banks, shall constitute the European System of Central Banks. The European Central Bank, together with the national central banks of the Member States whose currency is the euro, which constitute the Eurosystem, shall conduct the monetary policy of the Union.

2.   The European System of Central Banks shall be governed by the decision-making bodies of the European Central Bank. The primary objective of the European System of Central Banks shall be to maintain price stability. Without prejudice to that objective, it shall support the general economic policies in the Union in order to contribute to the achievement of the latter's objectives. It shall conduct other Central Bank tasks in accordance with Part III and the Statute of the European System of Central Banks and of the European Central Bank.

3.   The European Central Bank is an institution. It shall have legal personality. It alone may authorise the issue of the euro. It shall be independent in the exercise of its powers and in the management of its finances. Union institutions, bodies, offices and agencies and the governments of the Member States shall respect that independence.

4.   The European Central Bank shall adopt such measures as are necessary to carry out its tasks in accordance with Articles III-185 to III-191 and Article III-196, and with the conditions laid down in the Statute of the European System of Central Banks and of the European Central Bank. In accordance with these same Articles, those Member States whose currency is not the euro, and their central banks, shall retain their powers in monetary matters.

5.   Within the areas falling within its responsibilities, the European Central Bank shall be consulted on all proposed Union acts, and all proposals for regulation at national level, and may give an opinion.

6.   The decision-making organs of the European Central Bank, their composition and operating methods are set out in Articles III-382 and III-383, as well as in the Statute of the European System of Central Banks and of the European Central Bank.

ARTICLE I-31

The Court of Auditors

1.   The Court of Auditors is an institution. It shall carry out the Union's audit.

2.   It shall examine the accounts of all Union revenue and expenditure, and shall ensure good financial management.

3.   It shall consist of one national of each Member State. Its members shall be completely independent in the performance of their duties, in the Union's general interest.

ARTICLE I-32

The Union's advisory bodies

1.   The European Parliament, the Council and the Commission shall be assisted by a Committee of the Regions and an Economic and Social Committee, exercising advisory functions.

2.   The Committee of the Regions shall consist of representatives of regional and local bodies who either hold a regional or local authority electoral mandate or are politically accountable to an elected assembly.

3.   The Economic and Social Committee shall consist of representatives of organisations of employers, of the employed, and of other parties representative of civil society, notably in socio-economic, civic, professional and cultural areas.

4.   The members of the Committee of the Regions and the Economic and Social Committee shall not be bound by any mandatory instructions. They shall be completely independent in the performance of their duties, in the Union's general interest.

5.   Rules governing the composition of these Committees, the designation of their members, their powers and their operations are set out in Articles III-386 to III-392.

The rules referred to in paragraphs 2 and 3 governing the nature of their composition shall be reviewed at regular intervals by the Council to take account of economic, social and demographic developments within the Union. The Council, on a proposal from the Commission, shall adopt European decisions to that end.

TITLE V

EXERCISE OF UNION COMPETENCE

CHAPTER I

COMMON PROVISIONS

ARTICLE I-33

The legal acts of the Union

1.   To exercise the Union's competences the institutions shall use as legal instruments, in accordance with Part III, European laws, European framework laws, European regulations, European decisions, recommendations and opinions.

A European law shall be a legislative act of general application. It shall be binding in its entirety and directly applicable in all Member States.

A European framework law shall be a legislative act binding, as to the result to be achieved, upon each Member State to which it is addressed, but shall leave to the national authorities the choice of form and methods.

A European regulation shall be a non-legislative act of general application for the implementation of legislative acts and of certain provisions of the Constitution. It may either be binding in its entirety and directly applicable in all Member States, or be binding, as to the result to be achieved, upon each Member State to which it is addressed, but shall leave to the national authorities the choice of form and methods.

A European decision shall be a non-legislative act, binding in its entirety. A decision which specifies those to whom it is addressed shall be binding only on them.

Recommendations and opinions shall have no binding force.

2.   When considering draft legislative acts, the European Parliament and the Council shall refrain from adopting acts not provided for by the relevant legislative procedure in the area in question.

ARTICLE I-34

Legislative acts

1.   European laws and framework laws shall be adopted, on the basis of proposals from the Commission, jointly by the European Parliament and the Council under the ordinary legislative procedure as set out in Article III-396. If the two institutions cannot reach agreement on an act, it shall not be adopted.

2.   In the specific cases provided for in the Constitution, European laws and framework laws shall be adopted by the European Parliament with the participation of the Council, or by the

latter with the participation of the European Parliament, in accordance with special legislative procedures.

3.   In the specific cases provided for in the Constitution, European laws and framework laws may be adopted at the initiative of a group of Member States or of the European Parliament, on a recommendation from the European Central Bank or at the request of the Court of Justice or the European Investment Bank.

ARTICLE I-35

Non-legislative acts

1.   The European Council shall adopt European decisions in the cases provided for in the Constitution.

2.   The Council and the Commission, in particular in the cases referred to in Articles I–36 and I-37, and the European Central Bank in the specific cases provided for in the Constitution, shall adopt European regulations and decisions.

3.   The Council shall adopt recommendations. It shall act on a proposal from the Commission in all cases where the Constitution provides that it shall adopt acts on a proposal from the Commission. It shall act unanimously in those areas in which unanimity is required for the adoption of a Union act. The Commission, and the European Central Bank in the specific cases provided for in the Constitution, shall adopt recommendations.

ARTICLE I-36

Delegated European regulations

1.   European laws and framework laws may delegate to the Commission the power to adopt delegated European regulations to supplement or amend certain non-essential elements of the law or framework law.

The objectives, content, scope and duration of the delegation of power shall be explicitly defined in the European laws and framework laws. The essential elements of an area shall be reserved for the European law or framework law and accordingly shall not be the subject of a delegation of power.

2.   European laws and framework laws shall explicitly lay down the conditions to which the delegation is subject; these conditions may be as follows:

(a)   the European Parliament or the Council may decide to revoke the delegation;

(b)   the delegated European regulation may enter into force only if no objection has been expressed by the European Parliament or the Council within a period set by the European law or framework law.

For the purposes of (a) and (b), the European Parliament shall act by a majority of its component members, and the Council by a qualified majority.

ARTICLE I-37

Implementing acts

1.   Member States shall adopt all measures of national law necessary to implement legally binding Union acts.

2.   Where uniform conditions for implementing legally binding Union acts are needed, those acts shall confer implementing powers on the Commission, or, in duly justified specific cases and in the cases provided for in Article I-40, on the Council.

3.   For the purposes of paragraph 2, European laws shall lay down in advance the rules and general principles concerning mechanisms for control by Member States of the Commission's exercise of implementing powers.

4.   Union implementing acts shall take the form of European implementing regulations or European implementing decisions.

ARTICLE I-38

Principles common to the Union's legal acts

1.   Where the Constitution does not specify the type of act to be adopted, the institutions shall select it on a case-by-case basis, in compliance with the applicable procedures and with the principle of proportionality referred to in Article I-11.

2.   Legal acts shall state the reasons on which they are based and shall refer to any proposals, initiatives, recommendations, requests or opinions required by the Constitution.

ARTICLE I-39

Publication and entry into force

1.   European laws and framework laws adopted under the ordinary legislative procedure shall be signed by the President of the European Parliament and by the President of the Council.

In other cases they shall be signed by the President of the institution which adopted them.

European laws and framework laws shall be published in the Official Journal of the European Union and shall enter into force on the date specified in them or, in the absence thereof, on the twentieth day following their publication.

2.   European regulations, and European decisions which do not specify to whom they are addressed, shall be signed by the President of the institution which adopted them.

European regulations, and European decisions when the latter do not specify to whom they are addressed, shall be published in the Official Journal of the European Union and shall enter into force on the date specified in them or, in the absence thereof, on the twentieth day following that of their publication.

3.   European decisions other than those referred to in paragraph 2 shall be notified to those to whom they are addressed and shall take effect upon such notification.

CHAPTER II

SPECIFIC PROVISIONS

ARTICLE I-40

Specific provisions relating to the common foreign and security policy

1.   The European Union shall conduct a common foreign and security policy, based on the development of mutual political solidarity among Member States, the identification of questions of general interest and the achievement of an ever-increasing degree of convergence of Member States' actions.

2.   The European Council shall identify the Union's strategic interests and determine the objectives of its common foreign and security policy. The Council shall frame this policy within the framework of the strategic guidelines established by the European Council and in accordance with Part III.

3.   The European Council and the Council shall adopt the necessary European decisions.

4.   The common foreign and security policy shall be put into effect by the Union Minister for Foreign Affairs and by the Member States, using national and Union resources.

5.   Member States shall consult one another within the European Council and the Council on any foreign and security policy issue which is of general interest in order to determine a common approach. Before undertaking any action on the international scene or any commitment which could affect the Union's interests, each Member State shall consult the others within the European Council or the Council. Member States shall ensure, through the convergence of their actions, that the Union is able to assert its interests and values on the international scene. Member States shall show mutual solidarity.

6.   European decisions relating to the common foreign and security policy shall be adopted by the European Council and the Council unanimously, except in the cases referred to in Part III. The European Council and the Council shall act on an initiative from a Member State, on a proposal from the Union Minister for Foreign Affairs or on a proposal from that Minister with the Commission's support. European laws and framework laws shall be excluded.

7.   The European Council may, unanimously, adopt a European decision authorising the Council to act by a qualified majority in cases other than those referred to in Part III.

8.   The European Parliament shall be regularly consulted on the main aspects and basic choices of the common foreign and security policy. It shall be kept informed of how it evolves.

ARTICLE I-41

Specific provisions relating to the common security and defence policy

1. The common security and defence policy shall be an integral part of the common foreign and security policy. It shall provide the Union with an operational capacity drawing on civil and military assets. The Union may use them on missions outside the Union for peace-keeping, conflict prevention and strengthening international security in accordance with the principles of the United Nations Charter. The performance of these tasks shall be undertaken using capabilities provided by the Member States.

2. The common security and defence policy shall include the progressive framing of a common Union defence policy. This will lead to a common defence, when the European Council, acting unanimously, so decides. It shall in that case recommend to the Member States the adoption of such a decision in accordance with their respective constitutional requirements.

The policy of the Union in accordance with this Article shall not prejudice the specific character of the security and defence policy of certain Member States, it shall respect the obligations of certain Member States, which see their common defence realised in the North Atlantic Treaty Organisation, under the North Atlantic Treaty, and be compatible with the common security and defence policy established within that framework.

3. Member States shall make civilian and military capabilities available to the Union for the implementation of the common security and defence policy, to contribute to the objectives defined by the Council. Those Member States which together establish multinational forces may also make them available to the common security and defence policy.

Member States shall undertake progressively to improve their military capabilities. An Agency in the field of defence capabilities development, research, acquisition and armaments (European Defence Agency) shall be established to identify operational requirements, to promote measures to satisfy those requirements, to contribute to identifying and, where appropriate, implementing any measure needed to strengthen the industrial and technological base of the defence sector, to participate in defining a European capabilities and armaments policy, and to assist the Council in evaluating the improvement of military capabilities.

4. European decisions relating to the common security and defence policy, including those initiating a mission as referred to in this Article, shall be adopted by the Council acting unanimously on a proposal from the Union Minister for Foreign Affairs or an initiative from a Member State. The Union Minister for Foreign Affairs may propose the use of both national resources and Union instruments, together with the Commission where appropriate.

5. The Council may entrust the execution of a task, within the Union framework, to a group of Member States in order to protect the Union's values and serve its interests. The execution of such a task shall be governed by Article III-310.

6. Those Member States whose military capabilities fulfil higher criteria and which have made more binding commitments to one another in this area with a view to the most demanding missions shall establish permanent structured cooperation within the Union framework. Such cooperation shall be governed by Article III-312. It shall not affect the provisions of Article III-309.

7.   If a Member State is the victim of armed aggression on its territory, the other Member States shall have towards it an obligation of aid and assistance by all the means in their power, in accordance with Article 51 of the United Nations Charter. This shall not prejudice the specific character of the security and defence policy of certain Member States.

Commitments and cooperation in this area shall be consistent with commitments under the North Atlantic Treaty Organisation, which, for those States which are members of it, remains the foundation of their collective defence and the forum for its implementation.

8.   The European Parliament shall be regularly consulted on the main aspects and basic choices of the common security and defence policy. It shall be kept informed of how it evolves.

ARTICLE I-42

Specific provisions relating to the area of freedom, security and justice

1.   The Union shall constitute an area of freedom, security and justice:

(a)   by adopting European laws and framework laws intended, where necessary, to approximate laws and regulations of the Member States in the areas referred to in Part III;

(b)   by promoting mutual confidence between the competent authorities of the Member States, in particular on the basis of mutual recognition of judicial and extrajudicial decisions;

(c)   by operational cooperation between the competent authorities of the Member States, including the police, customs and other services specialising in the prevention and detection of criminal offences.

2.   National Parliaments may, within the framework of the area of freedom, security and justice, participate in the evaluation mechanisms provided for in Article III-260. They shall be involved in the political monitoring of Europol and the evaluation of Eurojust's activities in accordance with Articles III-276 and III-273.

3.   Member States shall have a right of initiative in the field of police and judicial cooperation in criminal matters, in accordance with Article III-264.

ARTICLE I-43

Solidarity clause

1.   The Union and its Member States shall act jointly in a spirit of solidarity if a Member State is the object of a terrorist attack or the victim of a natural or man-made disaster. The Union shall mobilise all the instruments at its disposal, including the military resources made available by the Member States, to:

(a)   –   prevent the terrorist threat in the territory of the Member States;

        –   protect democratic institutions and the civilian population from any terrorist attack;

–   assist a Member State in its territory, at the request of its political authorities, in the event of a terrorist attack;

(b)   assist a Member State in its territory, at the request of its political authorities, in the event of a natural or man-made disaster.

2.   The detailed arrangements for implementing this Article are set out in Article III-329.

CHAPTER III

ENHANCED COOPERATION

ARTICLE I-44

Enhanced cooperation

1.   Member States which wish to establish enhanced cooperation between themselves within the framework of the Union's non-exclusive competences may make use of its institutions and exercise those competences by applying the relevant provisions of the Constitution, subject to the limits and in accordance with the procedures laid down in this Article and in Articles III-416 to III-423.

Enhanced cooperation shall aim to further the objectives of the Union, protect its interests and reinforce its integration process. Such cooperation shall be open at any time to all Member States, in accordance with Article III-418.

2.   The European decision authorising enhanced cooperation shall be adopted by the Council as a last resort, when it has established that the objectives of such cooperation cannot be attained within a reasonable period by the Union as a whole, and provided that at least one third of the Member States participate in it. The Council shall act in accordance with the procedure laid down in Article III-419.

3.   All members of the Council may participate in its deliberations, but only members of the Council representing the Member States participating in enhanced cooperation shall take part in the vote.

Unanimity shall be constituted by the votes of the representatives of the participating Member States only.

A qualified majority shall be defined as at least 55% of the members of the Council representing the participating Member States, comprising at least 65% of the population of these States.

A blocking minority must include at least the minimum number of Council members representing more than 35% of the population of the participating Member States, plus one member, failing which the qualified majority shall be deemed attained.

By way of derogation from the third and fourth subparagraphs, where the Council does not act on a proposal from the Commission or from the Union Minister for Foreign Affairs, the required qualified majority shall be defined as at least 72% of the members of the Council representing the participating Member States, comprising at least 65% of the population of these States.

4.   Acts adopted in the framework of enhanced cooperation shall bind only participating Member States. They shall not be regarded as part of the *acquis* which has to be accepted by candidate States for accession to the Union.

TITLE VI

THE DEMOCRATIC LIFE OF THE UNION

ARTICLE I-45

The principle of democratic equality

In all its activities, the Union shall observe the principle of the equality of its citizens, who shall receive equal attention from its institutions, bodies, offices and agencies.

ARTICLE I-46

The principle of representative democracy

1.   The functioning of the Union shall be founded on representative democracy.

2.   Citizens are directly represented at Union level in the European Parliament.

Member States are represented in the European Council by their Heads of State or Government and in the Council by their governments, themselves democratically accountable either to their national Parliaments, or to their citizens.

3.   Every citizen shall have the right to participate in the democratic life of the Union. Decisions shall be taken as openly and as closely as possible to the citizen.

4.   Political parties at European level contribute to forming European political awareness and to expressing the will of citizens of the Union.

ARTICLE I-47

The principle of participatory democracy

1.   The institutions shall, by appropriate means, give citizens and representative associations the opportunity to make known and publicly exchange their views in all areas of Union action.

2.   The institutions shall maintain an open, transparent and regular dialogue with representative associations and civil society.

3.   The Commission shall carry out broad consultations with parties concerned in order to ensure that the Union's actions are coherent and transparent.

4.   Not less than one million citizens who are nationals of a significant number of Member States may take the initiative of inviting the Commission, within the framework of its powers, to submit any appropriate proposal on matters where citizens consider that a legal

act of the Union is required for the purpose of implementing the Constitution. European laws shall determine the provisions for the procedures and conditions required for such a citizens' initiative, including the minimum number of Member States from which such citizens must come.

ARTICLE I-48

The social partners and autonomous social dialogue

The Union recognises and promotes the role of the social partners at its level, taking into account the diversity of national systems. It shall facilitate dialogue between the social partners, respecting their autonomy.

The Tripartite Social Summit for Growth and Employment shall contribute to social dialogue.

ARTICLE I-49

The European Ombudsman

A European Ombudsman elected by the European Parliament shall receive, examine and report on complaints about maladministration in the activities of the Union institutions, bodies, offices or agencies, under the conditions laid down in the Constitution. The European Ombudsman shall be completely independent in the performance of his or her duties.

ARTICLE I-50

Transparency of the proceedings of Union institutions, bodies, offices and agencies

1.   In order to promote good governance and ensure the participation of civil society, the Union institutions, bodies, offices and agencies shall conduct their work as openly as possible.

2.   The European Parliament shall meet in public, as shall the Council when considering and voting on a draft legislative act.

3.   Any citizen of the Union, and any natural or legal person residing or having its registered office in a Member State shall have, under the conditions laid down in Part III, a right of access to documents of the Union institutions, bodies, offices and agencies, whatever their medium.

European laws shall lay down the general principles and limits which, on grounds of public or private interest, govern the right of access to such documents.

4.   Each institution, body, office or agency shall determine in its own rules of procedure specific provisions regarding access to its documents, in accordance with the European laws referred to in paragraph 3.

ARTICLE I-51

Protection of personal data

1. Everyone has the right to the protection of personal data concerning him or her.

2. European laws or framework laws shall lay down the rules relating to the protection of individuals with regard to the processing of personal data by Union institutions, bodies, offices and agencies, and by the Member States when carrying out activities which fall within the scope of Union law, and the rules relating to the free movement of such data. Compliance with these rules shall be subject to the control of independent authorities.

ARTICLE I-52

Status of churches and non-confessional organisations

1. The Union respects and does not prejudice the status under national law of churches and religious associations or communities in the Member States.

2. The Union equally respects the status under national law of philosophical and non-confessional organisations.

3. Recognising their identity and their specific contribution, the Union shall maintain an open, transparent and regular dialogue with these churches and organisations.

TITLE VII

THE UNION'S FINANCES

ARTICLE I-53

Budgetary and financial principles

1. All items of Union revenue and expenditure shall be included in estimates drawn up for each financial year and shall be shown in the Union's budget, in accordance with Part III.

2. The revenue and expenditure shown in the budget shall be in balance.

3. The expenditure shown in the budget shall be authorised for the annual budgetary period in accordance with the European law referred to in Article III-412.

4. The implementation of expenditure shown in the budget shall require the prior adoption of a legally binding Union act providing a legal basis for its action and for the implementation of the corresponding expenditure in accordance with the European law referred to in Article III-412, except in cases for which that law provides.

5. With a view to maintaining budgetary discipline, the Union shall not adopt any act which is likely to have appreciable implications for the budget without providing an assurance that the expenditure arising from such an act is capable of being financed within the limit of the

Union's own resources and in compliance with the multiannual financial framework referred to in Article I-55.

6.   The budget shall be implemented in accordance with the principle of sound financial management. Member States shall cooperate with the Union to ensure that the appropriations entered in the budget are used in accordance with this principle.

7.   The Union and the Member States, in accordance with Article III–415, shall counter fraud and any other illegal activities affecting the financial interests of the Union.

ARTICLE I-54

The Union's own resources

1.   The Union shall provide itself with the means necessary to attain its objectives and carry through its policies.

2.   Without prejudice to other revenue, the Union's budget shall be financed wholly from its own resources.

3.   A European law of the Council shall lay down the provisions relating to the system of own resources of the Union. In this context it may establish new categories of own resources or abolish an existing category. The Council shall act unanimously after consulting the European Parliament. That law shall not enter into force until it is approved by the Member States in accordance with their respective constitutional requirements.

4.   A European law of the Council shall lay down implementing measures of the Union's own resources system insofar as this is provided for in the European law adopted on the basis of paragraph 3. The Council shall act after obtaining the consent of the European Parliament.

ARTICLE I-55

The multiannual financial framework

1.   The multiannual financial framework shall ensure that Union expenditure develops in an orderly manner and within the limits of its own resources. It shall determine the amounts of the annual ceilings of appropriations for commitments by category of expenditure in accordance with Article III-402.

2.   A European law of the Council shall lay down the multiannual financial framework. The Council shall act unanimously after obtaining the consent of the European Parliament, which shall be given by a majority of its component members.

3.   The annual budget of the Union shall comply with the multiannual financial framework.

4.   The European Council may, unanimously, adopt a European decision authorising the Council to act by a qualified majority when adopting the European law of the Council referred to in paragraph 2.

ARTICLE I-56

The Union's budget

A European law shall establish the Union's annual budget in accordance with Article III-404.

TITLE VIII

THE UNION AND ITS NEIGHBOURS

ARTICLE I-57

The Union and its neighbours

1.   The Union shall develop a special relationship with neighbouring countries, aiming to establish an area of prosperity and good neighbourliness, founded on the values of the Union and characterised by close and peaceful relations based on cooperation.

2.   For the purposes of paragraph 1, the Union may conclude specific agreements with the countries concerned. These agreements may contain reciprocal rights and obligations as well as the possibility of undertaking activities jointly. Their implementation shall be the subject of periodic consultation.

TITLE IX

UNION MEMBERSHIP

ARTICLE I-58

Conditions of eligibility and procedure for accession to the Union

1.   The Union shall be open to all European States which respect the values referred to in Article I-2, and are committed to promoting them together.

2.   Any European State which wishes to become a member of the Union shall address its application to the Council. The European Parliament and national Parliaments shall be notified of this application. The Council shall act unanimously after consulting the Commission and after obtaining the consent of the European Parliament, which shall act by a majority of its component members. The conditions and arrangements for admission shall be the subject of an agreement between the Member States and the candidate State. That agreement shall be subject to ratification by each contracting State, in accordance with its respective constitutional requirements.

ARTICLE I-59

Suspension of certain rights resulting from Union membership

1.   On the reasoned initiative of one third of the Member States or the reasoned initiative of the European Parliament or on a proposal from the Commission, the Council may adopt a European decision determining that there is a clear risk of a serious breach by a Member State of the values referred to in Article I-2. The Council shall act by a majority of four fifths of its members after obtaining the consent of the European Parliament.

Before making such a determination, the Council shall hear the Member State in question and, acting in accordance with the same procedure, may address recommendations to that State.

The Council shall regularly verify that the grounds on which such a determination was made continue to apply.

2.   The European Council, on the initiative of one third of the Member States or on a proposal from the Commission, may adopt a European decision determining the existence of a serious and persistent breach by a Member State of the values mentioned in Article I-2, after inviting the Member State in question to submit its observations. The European Council shall act unanimously after obtaining the consent of the European Parliament.

3.   Where a determination under paragraph 2 has been made, the Council, acting by a qualified majority, may adopt a European decision suspending certain of the rights deriving from the application of the Constitution to the Member State in question, including the voting rights of the member of the Council representing that State. The Council shall take into account the possible consequences of such a suspension for the rights and obligations of natural and legal persons.

In any case, that State shall continue to be bound by its obligations under the Constitution.

4.   The Council, acting by a qualified majority, may adopt a European decision varying or revoking measures adopted under paragraph 3 in response to changes in the situation which led to their being imposed.

5.   For the purposes of this Article, the member of the European Council or of the Council representing the Member State in question shall not take part in the vote and the Member State in question shall not be counted in the calculation of the one third or four fifths of Member States referred to in paragraphs 1 and 2. Abstentions by members present in person or represented shall not prevent the adoption of European decisions referred to in paragraph 2.

For the adoption of the European decisions referred to in paragraphs 3 and 4, a qualified majority shall be defined as at least 72% of the members of the Council, representing the participating Member States, comprising at least 65% of the population of these States.

Where, following a decision to suspend voting rights adopted pursuant to paragraph 3, the Council acts by a qualified majority on the basis of a provision of the Constitution, that qualified majority shall be defined as in the second subparagraph, or, where the Council acts on a proposal from the Commission or from the Union Minister for Foreign Affairs, as at least 55% of the members of the Council representing the participating Member States, comprising at least 65% of the population of these States. In the latter case, a blocking minority must include at least the minimum number of Council members representing more than 35% of the population of the participating Member States, plus one member, failing which the qualified majority shall be deemed attained.

6.   For the purposes of this Article, the European Parliament shall act by a two-thirds majority of the votes cast, representing the majority of its component members.

ARTICLE I-60

Voluntary withdrawal from the Union

1.   Any Member State may decide to withdraw from the Union in accordance with its own constitutional requirements.

2.   A Member State which decides to withdraw shall notify the European Council of its intention. In the light of the guidelines provided by the European Council, the Union shall negotiate and conclude an agreement with that State, setting out the arrangements for its withdrawal, taking account of the framework for its future relationship with the Union. That agreement shall be negotiated in accordance with Article III-325(3). It shall be concluded by the Council, acting by a qualified majority, after obtaining the consent of the European Parliament.

3.   The Constitution shall cease to apply to the State in question from the date of entry into force of the withdrawal agreement or, failing that, two years after the notification referred to in paragraph 2, unless the European Council, in agreement with the Member State concerned, unanimously decides to extend this period.

4.   For the purposes of paragraphs 2 and 3, the member of the European Council or of the Council representing the withdrawing Member State shall not participate in the discussions of the European Council or Council or in European decisions concerning it.

A qualified majority shall be defined as at least 72% of the members of the Council, representing the participating Member States, comprising at least 65% of the population of these States.

5.   If a State which has withdrawn from the Union asks to rejoin, its request shall be subject to the procedure referred to in Article I-58.

PART II

THE CHARTER OF FUNDAMENTAL RIGHTS OF THE UNION

PREAMBLE

The peoples of Europe, in creating an ever closer union among them, are resolved to share a peaceful future based on common values.

Conscious of its spiritual and moral heritage, the Union is founded on the indivisible, universal values of human dignity, freedom, equality and solidarity; it is based on the principles of democracy and the rule of law. It places the individual at the heart of its activities, by establishing the citizenship of the Union and by creating an area of freedom, security and justice.

The Union contributes to the preservation and to the development of these common values while respecting the diversity of the cultures and traditions of the peoples of Europe as well as the national identities of the Member States and the organisation of their public authorities at national, regional and local levels; it seeks to promote balanced and sustainable development and ensures free movement of persons, services, goods and capital, and the freedom of establishment.

To this end, it is necessary to strengthen the protection of fundamental rights in the light of changes in society, social progress and scientific and technological developments by making those rights more visible in a Charter.

This Charter reaffirms, with due regard for the powers and tasks of the Union and the principle of subsidiarity, the rights as they result, in particular, from the constitutional traditions and international obligations common to the Member States, the European Convention for the Protection of Human Rights and Fundamental Freedoms, the Social Charters adopted by the Union and by the Council of Europe and the case law of the Court of Justice of the European Union and of the European Court of Human Rights. In this context the Charter will be interpreted by the courts of the Union and the Member States with due regard to the explanations prepared under the authority of the Praesidium of the Convention which drafted the Charter and updated under the responsibility of the Praesidium of the European Convention.

Enjoyment of these rights entails responsibilities and duties with regard to other persons, to the human community and to future generations.

The Union therefore recognises the rights, freedoms and principles set out hereafter.

TITLE I

DIGNITY

ARTICLE II-61

Human dignity

Human dignity is inviolable. It must be respected and protected.

ARTICLE II-62

Right to life

1.   Everyone has the right to life.

2.   No one shall be condemned to the death penalty, or executed.

ARTICLE II-63

Right to the integrity of the person

1.   Everyone has the right to respect for his or her physical and mental integrity.

2.   In the fields of medicine and biology, the following must be respected in particular:

(a)   the free and informed consent of the person concerned, according to the procedures laid down by law;

(b)   the prohibition of eugenic practices, in particular those aiming at the selection of persons;

(c)   the prohibition on making the human body and its parts as such a source of financial gain;

(d)   the prohibition of the reproductive cloning of human beings.

ARTICLE II-64

Prohibition of torture and inhuman or degrading treatment or punishment

No one shall be subjected to torture or to inhuman or degrading treatment or punishment.

ARTICLE II-65

Prohibition of slavery and forced labour

1.   No one shall be held in slavery or servitude.

2.   No one shall be required to perform forced or compulsory labour.

3.   Trafficking in human beings is prohibited.

TITLE II

FREEDOMS

ARTICLE II-66

Right to liberty and security

Everyone has the right to liberty and security of person.

ARTICLE II-67

Respect for private and family life

Everyone has the right to respect for his or her private and family life, home and communications.

ARTICLE II-68

Protection of personal data

1.   Everyone has the right to the protection of personal data concerning him or her.

2.   Such data must be processed fairly for specified purposes and on the basis of the consent of the person concerned or some other legitimate basis laid down by law. Everyone has the right of access to data which has been collected concerning him or her, and the right to have it rectified.

3.   Compliance with these rules shall be subject to control by an independent authority.

ARTICLE II-69

Right to marry and right to found a family

The right to marry and the right to found a family shall be guaranteed in accordance with the national laws governing the exercise of these rights.

ARTICLE II-70

Freedom of thought, conscience and religion

1.   Everyone has the right to freedom of thought, conscience and religion. This right includes freedom to change religion or belief and freedom, either alone or in community with others and in public or in private, to manifest religion or belief, in worship, teaching, practice and observance.

2.   The right to conscientious objection is recognised, in accordance with the national laws governing the exercise of this right.

ARTICLE II-71

Freedom of expression and information

1.   Everyone has the right to freedom of expression. This right shall include freedom to hold opinions and to receive and impart information and ideas without interference by public authority and regardless of frontiers.

2.   The freedom and pluralism of the media shall be respected.

ARTICLE II-72

Freedom of assembly and of association

1.   Everyone has the right to freedom of peaceful assembly and to freedom of association at all levels, in particular in political, trade union and civic matters, which implies the right of everyone to form and to join trade unions for the protection of his or her interests.

2.   Political parties at Union level contribute to expressing the political will of the citizens of the Union.

ARTICLE II-73

Freedom of the arts and sciences

The arts and scientific research shall be free of constraint. Academic freedom shall be respected.

ARTICLE II-74

Right to education

1.   Everyone has the right to education and to have access to vocational and continuing training.

2.   This right includes the possibility to receive free compulsory education.

3.   The freedom to found educational establishments with due respect for democratic principles and the right of parents to ensure the education and teaching of their children in conformity with their religious, philosophical and pedagogical convictions shall be respected, in accordance with the national laws governing the exercise of such freedom and right.

ARTICLE II-75

Freedom to choose an occupation and right to engage in work

1.   Everyone has the right to engage in work and to pursue a freely chosen or accepted occupation.

2.   Every citizen of the Union has the freedom to seek employment, to work, to exercise the right of establishment and to provide services in any Member State.

3.   Nationals of third countries who are authorised to work in the territories of the Member States are entitled to working conditions equivalent to those of citizens of the Union.

ARTICLE II-76

Freedom to conduct a business

The freedom to conduct a business in accordance with Union law and national laws and practices is recognised.

ARTICLE II-77

Right to property

1.   Everyone has the right to own, use, dispose of and bequeath his or her lawfully acquired possessions. No one may be deprived of his or her possessions, except in the public interest and in the cases and under the conditions provided for by law, subject to fair compensation being paid in good time for their loss. The use of property may be regulated by law insofar as is necessary for the general interest.

2.   Intellectual property shall be protected.

ARTICLE II-78

Right to asylum

The right to asylum shall be guaranteed with due respect for the rules of the Geneva Convention of 28 July 1951 and the Protocol of 31 January 1967 relating to the status of refugees and in accordance with the Constitution.

ARTICLE II-79

Protection in the event of removal, expulsion or extradition

1.   Collective expulsions are prohibited.

2.   No one may be removed, expelled or extradited to a State where there is a serious risk that he or she would be subjected to the death penalty, torture or other inhuman or degrading treatment or punishment.

TITLE III

EQUALITY

ARTICLE II-80

Equality before the law

Everyone is equal before the law.

ARTICLE II-81

Non-discrimination

1.   Any discrimination based on any ground such as sex, race, colour, ethnic or social origin, genetic features, language, religion or belief, political or any other opinion, membership of a national minority, property, birth, disability, age or sexual orientation shall be prohibited.

2.   Within the scope of application of the Constitution and without prejudice to any of its specific provisions, any discrimination on grounds of nationality shall be prohibited.

ARTICLE II-82

Cultural, religious and linguistic diversity

The Union shall respect cultural, religious and linguistic diversity.

ARTICLE II-83

Equality between women and men

Equality between women and men must be ensured in all areas, including employment, work and pay.

The principle of equality shall not prevent the maintenance or adoption of measures providing for specific advantages in favour of the under-represented sex.

ARTICLE II-84

The rights of the child

1.   Children shall have the right to such protection and care as is necessary for their well-being. They may express their views freely. Such views shall be taken into consideration on matters which concern them in accordance with their age and maturity.

2.   In all actions relating to children, whether taken by public authorities or private institutions, the child's best interests must be a primary consideration.

3.   Every child shall have the right to maintain on a regular basis a personal relationship and direct contact with both his or her parents, unless that is contrary to his or her interests.

ARTICLE II-85

The rights of the elderly

The Union recognises and respects the rights of the elderly to lead a life of dignity and independence and to participate in social and cultural life.

ARTICLE II-86

Integration of persons with disabilities

The Union recognises and respects the right of persons with disabilities to benefit from measures designed to ensure their independence, social and occupational integration and participation in the life of the community.

TITLE IV

SOLIDARITY

ARTICLE II-87

Workers' right to information and consultation within the undertaking

Workers or their representatives must, at the appropriate levels, be guaranteed information and consultation in good time in the cases and under the conditions provided for by Union law and national laws and practices.

ARTICLE II-88

Right of collective bargaining and action

Workers and employers, or their respective organisations, have, in accordance with Union law and national laws and practices, the right to negotiate and conclude collective agreements at the appropriate levels and, in cases of conflicts of interest, to take collective action to defend their interests, including strike action.

ARTICLE II-89

Right of access to placement services

Everyone has the right of access to a free placement service.

ARTICLE II-90

Protection in the event of unjustified dismissal

Every worker has the right to protection against unjustified dismissal, in accordance with Union law and national laws and practices.

ARTICLE II-91

Fair and just working conditions

1.   Every worker has the right to working conditions which respect his or her health, safety and dignity.

2.   Every worker has the right to limitation of maximum working hours, to daily and weekly rest periods and to an annual period of paid leave.

ARTICLE II-92

Prohibition of child labour and protection of young people at work

The employment of children is prohibited. The minimum age of admission to employment may not be lower than the minimum school-leaving age, without prejudice to such rules as may be more favourable to young people and except for limited derogations.

Young people admitted to work must have working conditions appropriate to their age and be protected against economic exploitation and any work likely to harm their safety, health or physical, mental, moral or social development or to interfere with their education.

ARTICLE II-93

Family and professional life

1.   The family shall enjoy legal, economic and social protection.

2.   To reconcile family and professional life, everyone shall have the right to protection from dismissal for a reason connected with maternity and the right to paid maternity leave and to parental leave following the birth or adoption of a child.

ARTICLE II-94

Social security and social assistance

1.   The Union recognises and respects the entitlement to social security benefits and social services providing protection in cases such as maternity, illness, industrial accidents, dependency or old age, and in the case of loss of employment, in accordance with the rules laid down by Union law and national laws and practices.

2.   Everyone residing and moving legally within the European Union is entitled to social security benefits and social advantages in accordance with Union law and national laws and practices.

3.   In order to combat social exclusion and poverty, the Union recognises and respects the right to social and housing assistance so as to ensure a decent existence for all those who lack sufficient resources, in accordance with the rules laid down by Union law and national laws and practices.

ARTICLE II-95

Health care

Everyone has the right of access to preventive health care and the right to benefit from medical treatment under the conditions established by national laws and practices. A high level of human health protection shall be ensured in the definition and implementation of all Union policies and activities.

ARTICLE II-96

Access to services of general economic interest

The Union recognises and respects access to services of general economic interest as provided for in national laws and practices, in accordance with the Constitution, in order to promote the social and territorial cohesion of the Union.

ARTICLE II-97

Environmental protection

A high level of environmental protection and the improvement of the quality of the environment must be integrated into the policies of the Union and ensured in accordance with the principle of sustainable development.

ARTICLE II-98

Consumer protection

Union policies shall ensure a high level of consumer protection.

TITLE V

CITIZENS' RIGHTS

ARTICLE II-99

Right to vote and to stand as a candidate at elections to the European Parliament

1.   Every citizen of the Union has the right to vote and to stand as a candidate at elections to the European Parliament in the Member State in which he or she resides, under the same conditions as nationals of that State.

2.   Members of the European Parliament shall be elected by direct universal suffrage in a free and secret ballot.

ARTICLE II-100

Right to vote and to stand as a candidate at municipal elections

Every citizen of the Union has the right to vote and to stand as a candidate at municipal elections in the Member State in which he or she resides under the same conditions as nationals of that State.

ARTICLE II-101

Right to good administration

1.   Every person has the right to have his or her affairs handled impartially, fairly and within a reasonable time by the institutions, bodies, offices and agencies of the Union.

2.   This right includes:

(a)   the right of every person to be heard, before any individual measure which would affect him or her adversely is taken;

(b)   the right of every person to have access to his or her file, while respecting the legitimate interests of confidentiality and of professional and business secrecy;

(c)   the obligation of the administration to give reasons for its decisions.

3.   Every person has the right to have the Union make good any damage caused by its institutions or by its servants in the performance of their duties, in accordance with the general principles common to the laws of the Member States.

4.   Every person may write to the institutions of the Union in one of the languages of the Constitution and must have an answer in the same language.

ARTICLE II-102

Right of access to documents

Any citizen of the Union, and any natural or legal person residing or having its registered office in a Member State, has a right of access to documents of the institutions, bodies, offices and agencies of the Union, whatever their medium.

ARTICLE II-103

European Ombudsman

Any citizen of the Union and any natural or legal person residing or having its registered office in a Member State has the right to refer to the European Ombudsman cases of maladministration in the activities of the institutions, bodies, offices or agencies of the Union, with the exception of the Court of Justice of the European Union acting in its judicial role.

ARTICLE II-104

Right to petition

Any citizen of the Union and any natural or legal person residing or having its registered office in a Member State has the right to petition the European Parliament.

ARTICLE II-105

Freedom of movement and of residence

1.   Every citizen of the Union has the right to move and reside freely within the territory of the Member States.

2.   Freedom of movement and residence may be granted, in accordance with the Constitution, to nationals of third countries legally resident in the territory of a Member State.

ARTICLE II-106

Diplomatic and consular protection

Every citizen of the Union shall, in the territory of a third country in which the Member State of which he or she is a national is not represented, be entitled to protection by the diplomatic or consular authorities of any Member State, on the same conditions as the nationals of that Member State.

TITLE VI

JUSTICE

ARTICLE II-107

Right to an effective remedy and to a fair trial

Everyone whose rights and freedoms guaranteed by the law of the Union are violated has the right to an effective remedy before a tribunal in compliance with the conditions laid down in this Article.

Everyone is entitled to a fair and public hearing within a reasonable time by an independent and impartial tribunal previously established by law. Everyone shall have the possibility of being advised, defended and represented.

Legal aid shall be made available to those who lack sufficient resources insofar as such aid is necessary to ensure effective access to justice.

ARTICLE II-108

Presumption of innocence and right of defence

1.   Everyone who has been charged shall be presumed innocent until proved guilty according to law.

2.   Respect for the rights of the defence of anyone who has been charged shall be guaranteed.

ARTICLE II-109

Principles of legality and proportionality of criminal offences and penalties

1.   No one shall be held guilty of any criminal offence on account of any act or omission which did not constitute a criminal offence under national law or international law at the time when it was committed. Nor shall a heavier penalty be imposed than that which was applicable at the time the criminal offence was committed. If, subsequent to the commission of a criminal offence, the law provides for a lighter penalty, that penalty shall be applicable.

2.   This Article shall not prejudice the trial and punishment of any person for any act or omission which, at the time when it was committed, was criminal according to the general principles recognised by the community of nations.

3.   The severity of penalties must not be disproportionate to the criminal offence.

ARTICLE II-110

Right not to be tried or punished twice in criminal proceedings for the same criminal offence

No one shall be liable to be tried or punished again in criminal proceedings for an offence for which he or she has already been finally acquitted or convicted within the Union in accordance with the law.

TITLE VII

GENERAL PROVISIONS GOVERNING THE INTERPRETATION AND APPLICATION OF THE CHARTER

ARTICLE II-111

Field of application

1.   The provisions of this Charter are addressed to the institutions, bodies, offices and agencies of the Union with due regard for the principle of subsidiarity and to the Member States only when they are implementing Union law. They shall therefore respect the rights, observe the principles and promote the application thereof in accordance with their respective powers and respecting the limits of the powers of the Union as conferred on it in the other Parts of the Constitution.

2.   This Charter does not extend the field of application of Union law beyond the powers of the Union or establish any new power or task for the Union, or modify powers and tasks defined in the other Parts of the Constitution.

ARTICLE II-112

Scope and interpretation of rights and principles

1.   Any limitation on the exercise of the rights and freedoms recognised by this Charter must be provided for by law and respect the essence of those rights and freedoms. Subject to the principle of proportionality, limitations may be made only if they are necessary and genuinely meet objectives of general interest recognised by the Union or the need to protect the rights and freedoms of others.

2.   Rights recognised by this Charter for which provision is made in other Parts of the Constitution shall be exercised under the conditions and within the limits defined by these relevant Parts.

3.   Insofar as this Charter contains rights which correspond to rights guaranteed by the Convention for the Protection of Human Rights and Fundamental Freedoms, the meaning and scope of those rights shall be the same as those laid down by the said Convention. This provision shall not prevent Union law providing more extensive protection.

4.   Insofar as this Charter recognises fundamental rights as they result from the constitutional traditions common to the Member States, those rights shall be interpreted in harmony with those traditions.

5.   The provisions of this Charter which contain principles may be implemented by legislative and executive acts taken by institutions, bodies, offices and agencies of the Union, and by acts of Member States when they are implementing Union law, in the exercise of their respective powers. They shall be judicially cognisable only in the interpretation of such acts and in the ruling on their legality.

6.   Full account shall be taken of national laws and practices as specified in this Charter.

7.   The explanations drawn up as a way of providing guidance in the interpretation of the Charter of Fundamental Rights shall be given due regard by the courts of the Union and of the Member States.

ARTICLE II-113

Level of protection

Nothing in this Charter shall be interpreted as restricting or adversely affecting human rights and fundamental freedoms as recognised, in their respective fields of application, by Union law and international law and by international agreements to which the Union or all the Member States are party, including the European Convention for the Protection of Human Rights and Fundamental Freedoms, and by the Member States' constitutions.

ARTICLE II-114

Prohibition of abuse of rights

Nothing in this Charter shall be interpreted as implying any right to engage in any activity or to perform any act aimed at the destruction of any of the rights and freedoms recognised in this Charter or at their limitation to a greater extent than is provided for herein.

PART III

THE POLICIES AND FUNCTIONING OF THE UNION

TITLE I

PROVISIONS OF GENERAL APPLICATION

ARTICLE III-115

The Union shall ensure consistency between the policies and activities referred to in this Part, taking all of its objectives into account and in accordance with the principle of conferral of powers.

ARTICLE III-116

In all the activities referred to in this Part, the Union shall aim to eliminate inequalities, and to promote equality, between women and men.

ARTICLE III-117

In defining and implementing the policies and actions referred to in this Part, the Union shall take into account requirements linked to the promotion of a high level of employment, the guarantee of adequate social protection, the fight against social exclusion, and a high level of education, training and protection of human health.

ARTICLE III-118

In defining and implementing the policies and activities referred to in this Part, the Union shall aim to combat discrimination based on sex, racial or ethnic origin, religion or belief, disability, age or sexual orientation.

ARTICLE III-119

Environmental protection requirements must be integrated into the definition and implementation of the policies and activities referred to in this Part, in particular with a view to promoting sustainable development.

ARTICLE III-120

Consumer protection requirements shall be taken into account in defining and implementing other Union policies and activities.

ARTICLE III-121

In formulating and implementing the Union's agriculture, fisheries, transport, internal market, research and technological development and space policies, the Union and the Member States shall, since animals are sentient beings, pay full regard to the requirements of animal welfare, while respecting the legislative or administrative provisions and customs of Member States relating in particular to religious rites, cultural traditions and regional heritage.

ARTICLE III-122

Without prejudice to Articles I-5, III-166, III-167 and III-238, and given the place occupied by services of general economic interest as services to which all in the Union attribute value as well as their role in promoting its social and territorial cohesion, the Union and the Member States, each within their respective competences and within the scope of application of the Constitution, shall take care that such services operate on the basis of principles and conditions, in particular economic and financial conditions, which enable them to fulfil their missions. European laws shall establish these principles and set these conditions without prejudice to the competence of Member States, in compliance with the Constitution, to provide, to commission and to fund such services.

TITLE II

NON-DISCRIMINATION AND CITIZENSHIP

ARTICLE III-123

European laws or framework laws may lay down rules to prohibit discrimination on grounds of nationality as referred to in Article I-4(2).

ARTICLE III-124

1.   Without prejudice to the other provisions of the Constitution and within the limits of the powers assigned by it to the Union, a European law or framework law of the Council may establish the measures needed to combat discrimination based on sex, racial or ethnic origin, religion or belief, disability, age or sexual orientation. The Council shall act unanimously after obtaining the consent of the European Parliament.

2.   By way of derogation from paragraph 1, European laws or framework laws may establish basic principles for Union incentive measures and define such measures, to support action taken by Member States in order to contribute to the achievement of the objectives referred to in paragraph 1, excluding any harmonisation of their laws and regulations.

ARTICLE III-125

1.   If action by the Union should prove necessary to facilitate the exercise of the right, referred to in Article I-10(2)(a), of every citizen of the Union to move and reside freely and the Constitution has not provided the necessary powers, European laws or framework laws may establish measures for that purpose.

2.   For the same purposes as those referred to in paragraph 1 and if the Constitution has not provided the necessary powers, a European law or framework law of the Council may establish measures concerning passports, identity cards, residence permits or any other such document and measures concerning social security or social protection. The Council shall act unanimously after consulting the European Parliament.

ARTICLE III-126

A European law or framework law of the Council shall determine the detailed arrangements for exercising the right, referred to in Article I-10(2)(b), for every citizen of the Union to vote and to stand as a candidate in municipal elections and elections to the European Parliament in his or her Member State of residence without being a national of that State. The Council shall act unanimously after consulting the European Parliament. These arrangements may provide for derogations where warranted by problems specific to a Member State.

The right to vote and to stand as a candidate in elections to the European Parliament shall be exercised without prejudice to Article III-330(1) and the measures adopted for its implementation.

ARTICLE III-127

Member States shall adopt the necessary provisions to secure diplomatic and consular protection of citizens of the Union in third countries, as referred to in Article I-10(2)(c).

Member States shall commence the international negotiations required to secure this protection.

A European law of the Council may establish the measures necessary to facilitate such protection. The Council shall act after consulting the European Parliament.

ARTICLE III-128

The languages in which every citizen of the Union has the right to address the institutions or bodies under Article I-10(2)(d), and to have an answer, are those listed in Article IV-448(1). The institutions and bodies referred to in Article I-10(2)(d) are those listed in Articles I-19(1), second subparagraph, I-30, I-31 and I-32 and also the European Ombudsman.

ARTICLE III-129

The Commission shall report to the European Parliament, to the Council and to the Economic and Social Committee every three years on the application of Article I-10 and of this Title. This report shall take account of the development of the Union.

On the basis of this report, and without prejudice to the other provisions of the Constitution, a European law or framework law of the Council may add to the rights laid down in Article I-10. The Council shall act unanimously after obtaining the consent of the European Parliament. The law or framework law concerned shall not enter into force until it is approved by the Member States in accordance with their respective constitutional requirements.

TITLE III

INTERNAL POLICIES AND ACTION

CHAPTER I

INTERNAL MARKET

SECTION 1

ESTABLISHMENT AND FUNCTIONING OF THE INTERNAL MARKET

ARTICLE III-130

1.   The Union shall adopt measures with the aim of establishing or ensuring the functioning of the internal market, in accordance with the relevant provisions of the Constitution.

2.   The internal market shall comprise an area without internal frontiers in which the free movement of persons, services, goods and capital is ensured in accordance with the Constitution.

3.   The Council, on a proposal from the Commission, shall adopt European regulations and decisions determining the guidelines and conditions necessary to ensure balanced progress in all the sectors concerned.

4.   When drawing up its proposals for achieving the objectives set out in paragraphs 1 and 2, the Commission shall take into account the extent of the effort that certain economies showing differences in development will have to sustain for the establishment of the internal market and it may propose appropriate measures.

If these measures take the form of derogations, they must be of a temporary nature and must cause the least possible disturbance to the functioning of the internal market.

ARTICLE III-131

Member States shall consult each other with a view to taking together the steps needed to prevent the functioning of the internal market being affected by measures which a Member State may be called upon to take in the event of serious internal disturbances affecting the maintenance of law and order, in the event of war, serious international tension constituting a threat of war, or in order to carry out obligations it has accepted for the purpose of maintaining peace and international security.

ARTICLE III-132

If measures taken in the circumstances referred to in Articles III-131 and III-436 have the effect of distorting the conditions of competition in the internal market, the Commission shall, together with the Member State concerned, examine how these measures can be adjusted to the rules laid down in the Constitution.

By way of derogation from the procedure laid down in Articles III-360 and III-361, the Commission or any Member State may bring the matter directly before the Court of Justice if the Commission or Member State considers that another Member State is making improper use of the powers provided for in Articles III-131 and III-436. The Court of Justice shall give its ruling in camera.

SECTION 2

FREE MOVEMENT OF PERSONS AND SERVICES

Subsection 1

Workers

ARTICLE III-133

1.   Workers shall have the right to move freely within the Union.

2.   Any discrimination based on nationality between workers of the Member States as regards employment, remuneration and other conditions of work and employment shall be prohibited.

3.   Workers shall have the right, subject to limitations justified on grounds of public policy, public security or public health:

(a)   to accept offers of employment actually made;

(b)   to move freely within the territory of Member States for this purpose;

(c)   to stay in a Member State for the purpose of employment in accordance with the provisions governing the employment of nationals of that State laid down by law, regulation or administrative action;

(d)   to remain in the territory of a Member State after having been employed in that State, subject to conditions which shall be embodied in European regulations adopted by the Commission.

4.   This Article shall not apply to employment in the public service.

ARTICLE III-134

European laws or framework laws shall establish the measures needed to bring about freedom of movement for workers, as defined in Article III-133. They shall be adopted after consultation of the Economic and Social Committee.

Such European laws or framework laws shall aim, in particular, to:

(a)   ensure close cooperation between national employment services;

(b)   abolish those administrative procedures and practices and those qualifying periods in respect of eligibility for available employment, whether resulting from national legislation or from agreements previously concluded between Member States, the maintenance of which would form an obstacle to liberalisation of the movement of workers;

(c)   abolish all such qualifying periods and other restrictions provided for either under national legislation or under agreements previously concluded between Member States as impose on workers of other Member States conditions regarding the free choice of employment other than those imposed on workers of the State concerned;

(d)   set up appropriate machinery to bring offers of employment into touch with applications for employment and to facilitate the achievement of a balance between supply and demand in the employment market in such a way as to avoid serious threats to the standard of living and level of employment in the various regions and industries.

ARTICLE III-135

Member States shall, within the framework of a joint programme, encourage the exchange of young workers.

ARTICLE III-136

1.   In the field of social security, European laws or framework laws shall establish such measures as are necessary to bring about freedom of movement for workers by making arrangements to secure for employed and self-employed migrant workers and their dependants:

(a)   aggregation, for the purpose of acquiring and retaining the right to benefit and of calculating the amount of benefit, of all periods taken into account under the laws of the different countries;

(b)   payment of benefits to persons resident in the territories of Member States.

2.   Where a member of the Council considers that a draft European law or framework law referred to in paragraph 1 would affect fundamental aspects of its social security system, including its scope, cost or financial structure, or would affect the financial balance of that system, it may request that the matter be referred to the European Council. In that case, the procedure referred to in Article III-396 shall be suspended. After discussion, the European Council shall, within four months of this suspension, either:

(a)   refer the draft back to the Council, which shall terminate the suspension of the procedure referred to in Article III-396, or

(b)   request the Commission to submit a new proposal; in that case, the act originally proposed shall be deemed not to have been adopted.

Subsection 2
Freedom of establishment

ARTICLE III-137

Within the framework of this Subsection, restrictions on the freedom of establishment of nationals of a Member State in the territory of another Member State shall be prohibited. Such prohibition shall also apply to restrictions on the setting-up of agencies, branches or subsidiaries by nationals of any Member State established in the territory of any Member State.

Nationals of a Member State shall have the right, in the territory of another Member State, to take up and pursue activities as self-employed persons and to set up and manage undertakings, in particular companies or firms within the meaning of the second paragraph of Article III-142, under the conditions laid down for its own nationals by the law of the Member State where such establishment is effected, subject to Section 4 relating to capital and payments.

ARTICLE III-138

1.   European framework laws shall establish measures to attain freedom of establishment as regards a particular activity. They shall be adopted after consultation of the Economic and Social Committee.

2.   The European Parliament, the Council and the Commission shall carry out the duties devolving upon them under paragraph 1, in particular:

(a)   by according, as a general rule, priority treatment to activities where freedom of establishment makes a particularly valuable contribution to the development of production and trade;

(b)   by ensuring close cooperation between the competent authorities in the Member States in order to ascertain the particular situation within the Union of the various activities concerned;

(c)   by abolishing those administrative procedures and practices, whether resulting from national legislation or from agreements previously concluded between Member States, the maintenance of which would form an obstacle to freedom of establishment;

(d)   by ensuring that workers from one Member State employed in the territory of another Member State may remain in that territory for the purpose of taking up activities therein as self-employed persons, where they satisfy the conditions which they would be required to satisfy if they were entering that State at the time when they intended to take up such activities;

(e)   by enabling a national of one Member State to acquire and use land and buildings situated in the territory of another Member State, insofar as this does not conflict with the principles laid down in Article III-227(2);

(f)   by effecting the progressive abolition of restrictions on freedom of establishment in every branch of activity under consideration, both as regards the conditions for setting up agencies, branches or subsidiaries in the territory of a Member State and as regards the conditions governing the entry of personnel belonging to the main establishment into managerial or supervisory posts in such agencies, branches or subsidiaries;

(g)   by coordinating to the necessary extent the safeguards which, for the protection of the interests of members and others, are required by Member States of companies or firms within the meaning of the second paragraph of Article III-142 with a view to making such safeguards equivalent throughout the Union;

(h)   by satisfying themselves that the conditions of establishment are not distorted by aids granted by Member States.

ARTICLE III-139

This Subsection shall not apply, so far as any given Member State is concerned, to activities which in that State are connected, even occasionally, with the exercise of official authority.

European laws or framework laws may exclude certain activities from application of this Subsection.

ARTICLE III-140

1.   This Subsection and measures adopted in pursuance thereof shall not prejudice the applicability of provisions laid down by law, regulation or administrative action in Member States providing for special treatment for foreign nationals on grounds of public policy, public security or public health.

2.   European framework laws shall coordinate the national provisions referred to in paragraph 1.

ARTICLE III-141

1.   European framework laws shall make it easier for persons to take up and pursue activities as self-employed persons. They shall cover:

(a)   the mutual recognition of diplomas, certificates and other evidence of formal qualifications;

(b)   the coordination of the provisions laid down by law, regulation or administrative action in Member States concerning the taking-up and pursuit of activities as self-employed persons.

2.   In the case of the medical and allied and pharmaceutical professions, the progressive abolition of restrictions shall be dependent upon coordination of the conditions for the exercise of such professions in the various Member States.

ARTICLE III-142

Companies or firms formed in accordance with the law of a Member State and having their registered office, central administration or principal place of business within the Union shall, for the purposes of this Subsection, be treated in the same way as natural persons who are nationals of Member States.

"Companies or firms" means companies or firms constituted under civil or commercial law, including cooperative societies, and other legal persons governed by public or private law, save for those which are non-profit-making.

ARTICLE III-143

Member States shall accord nationals of the other Member States the same treatment as their own nationals as regards participation in the capital of companies or firms within the meaning of the second paragraph of Article III-142, without prejudice to the application of the other provisions of the Constitution.

Subsection 3
Freedom to provide services

ARTICLE III-144

Within the framework of this Subsection, restrictions on freedom to provide services within the Union shall be prohibited in respect of nationals of Member States who are established in a Member State other than that of the person for whom the services are intended.

European laws or framework laws may extend this Subsection to service providers who are nationals of a third State and who are established within the Union.

ARTICLE III-145

Services shall be considered to be "services" for the purposes of the Constitution where they are normally provided for remuneration, insofar as they are not governed by the provisions relating to freedom of movement for persons, goods and capital.

"Services" shall in particular include:

(a)   activities of an industrial character;

(b)   activities of a commercial character;

(c)   activities of craftsmen;

(d)   activities of the professions.

Without prejudice to Subsection 2 relating to freedom of establishment, the person providing a service may, in order to do so, temporarily pursue his or her activity in the Member State where the

service is provided, under the same conditions as are imposed by that State on its own nationals.

ARTICLE III-146

1.   Freedom to provide services in the field of transport shall be governed by Section 7 of Chapter III relating to transport.

2.   The liberalisation of banking and insurance services connected with movements of capital shall be effected in step with the liberalisation of movement of capital.

ARTICLE III-147

1.   European framework laws shall establish measures to achieve the liberalisation of a specific service. They shall be adopted after consultation of the Economic and Social Committee.

2.   European framework laws referred to in paragraph 1 shall as a general rule give priority to those services which directly affect production costs or the liberalisation of which helps to promote trade in goods.

ARTICLE III-148

The Member States shall endeavour to undertake liberalisation of services beyond the extent required by the European framework laws adopted pursuant to Article III-147(1), if their general economic situation and the situation of the economic sector concerned so permit.

To this end, the Commission shall make recommendations to the Member States concerned.

ARTICLE III-149

As long as restrictions on freedom to provide services have not been abolished, the Member States shall apply such restrictions without distinction on grounds of nationality or of residence to all persons providing services within the meaning of the first paragraph of Article III-144.

ARTICLE III-150

Articles III-139 to III-142 shall apply to the matters covered by this Subsection.

SECTION 3
FREE MOVEMENT OF GOODS

Subsection 1
Customs union

ARTICLE III-151

1.   The Union shall comprise a customs union which shall cover all trade in goods and which shall involve the prohibition between Member States of customs duties on imports and exports and of all charges having equivalent effect, and the adoption of a common customs tariff in their relations with third countries.

2.   Paragraph 4 and Subsection 3 on the prohibition of quantitative restrictions shall apply to products originating in Member States and to products coming from third countries which are in free circulation in Member States.

3.   Products coming from a third country shall be considered to be in free circulation in a Member State if the import formalities have been complied with and any customs duties or charges having equivalent effect which are payable have been levied in that Member State, and if they have not benefited from a total or partial drawback of such duties or charges.

4.   Customs duties on imports and exports and charges having equivalent effect shall be prohibited between Member States. This prohibition shall also apply to customs duties of a fiscal nature.

5.   The Council, on a proposal from the Commission, shall adopt the European regulations and decisions fixing Common Customs Tariff duties.

6.   In carrying out the tasks entrusted to it under this Article the Commission shall be guided by:

(a)   the need to promote trade between Member States and third countries;

(b)   developments in conditions of competition within the Union insofar as they lead to an improvement in the competitive capacity of undertakings;

(c)   the requirements of the Union as regards the supply of raw materials and semi-finished goods; in this connection the Commission shall take care to avoid distorting conditions of competition between Member States in respect of finished goods;

(d)   the need to avoid serious disturbances in the economies of Member States and to ensure rational development of production and an expansion of consumption within the Union.

Subsection 2

Customs cooperation

ARTICLE III-152

Within the scope of application of the Constitution, European laws or framework laws shall establish measures in order to strengthen customs cooperation between Member States and between them and the Commission.

Subsection 3

Prohibition of quantitative restrictions

ARTICLE III-153

Quantitative restrictions on imports and exports and all measures having equivalent effect shall be prohibited between Member States.

ARTICLE III-154

Article III-153 shall not preclude prohibitions or restrictions on imports, exports or goods in transit justified on grounds of public morality, public policy or public security; the protection of health and life of humans, animals or plants; the protection of national treasures possessing artistic, historic or archaeological value; or the protection of industrial and commercial property. Such prohibitions or restrictions shall not, however, constitute a means of arbitrary discrimination or a disguised restriction on trade between Member States.

ARTICLE III-155

1.   Member States shall adjust any State monopolies of a commercial character so as to ensure that no discrimination regarding the conditions under which goods are procured and marketed exists between nationals of Member States.

This Article shall apply to any body through which a Member State, in law or in fact, either directly or indirectly supervises, determines or appreciably influences imports or exports between Member States. It shall likewise apply to monopolies delegated by the State to others.

2.   Member States shall refrain from introducing any new measure which is contrary to the principles laid down in paragraph 1 or which restricts the scope of the Articles dealing with the prohibition of customs duties and quantitative restrictions between Member States.

3.   If a State monopoly of a commercial character has rules which are designed to make it easier to dispose of agricultural products or obtain for them the best return, steps should be taken in applying this Article to ensure equivalent safeguards for the employment and standard of living of the producers concerned.

SECTION 4

CAPITAL AND PAYMENTS

ARTICLE III-156

Within the framework of this Section, restrictions both on the movement of capital and on payments between Member States and between Member States and third countries shall be prohibited.

ARTICLE III-157

1.   Article III-156 shall be without prejudice to the application to third countries of any restrictions which existed on 31 December 1993 under national or Union law adopted in respect of the movement of capital to or from third countries involving direct investment – including investment in real estate, establishment, the provision of financial services or the admission of securities to capital markets. With regard to restrictions which exist under national law in Estonia and Hungary, the date in question shall be 31 December 1999.

2.   European laws or framework laws shall enact measures on the movement of capital to or from third countries involving direct investment – including investment in real estate, establishment, the provision of financial services or the admission of securities to capital markets.

The European Parliament and the Council shall endeavour to achieve the objective of free movement of capital between Member States and third countries to the greatest extent possible and without prejudice to other provisions of the Constitution.

3.   Notwithstanding paragraph 2, only a European law or framework law of the Council may enact measures which constitute a step backwards in Union law as regards the liberalisation of the movement of capital to or from third countries. The Council shall act unanimously after consulting the European Parliament.

ARTICLE III-158

1.   Article III-156 shall be without prejudice to the right of Member States:

(a)   to apply the relevant provisions of their tax law which distinguish between taxpayers who are not in the same situation with regard to their place of residence or with regard to the place where their capital is invested;

(b)   to take all requisite measures to prevent infringements of national provisions laid down by law or regulation, in particular in the field of taxation and the prudential supervision of financial institutions, or to lay down procedures for the declaration of capital movements for purposes of administrative or statistical information, or to take measures which are justified on grounds of public policy or public security.

2.   This Section shall be without prejudice to the applicability of restrictions on the right of establishment which are compatible with the Constitution.

3.   The measures and procedures referred to in paragraphs 1 and 2 shall not constitute a means of arbitrary discrimination or a disguised restriction on the free movement of capital and payments as defined in Article III-156.

4.   In the absence of a European law or framework law provided for in Article III-157(3), the Commission or, in the absence of a European decision of the Commission within three months from the request of the Member State concerned, the Council, may adopt a European decision stating that restrictive tax measures adopted by a Member State concerning one or more third countries are to be considered compatible with the Constitution insofar as they are justified by one of the objectives of the Union and compatible with the proper functioning of the internal market. The Council shall act unanimously on application by a Member State.

ARTICLE III-159

Where, in exceptional circumstances, movements of capital to or from third countries cause, or threaten to cause, serious difficulties for the functioning of economic and monetary union, the Council, on a proposal from the Commission, may adopt European regulations or decisions introducing safeguard measures with regard to third countries for a period not exceeding six months if such measures are strictly necessary. It shall act after consulting the European Central Bank.

ARTICLE III-160

Where necessary to achieve the objectives set out in Article III-257, as regards preventing and combating terrorism and related activities, European laws shall define a framework for administrative measures with regard to capital movements and payments, such as the freezing of funds, financial assets or economic gains belonging to, or owned or held by, natural or legal persons, groups or non-State entities.

The Council, on a proposal from the Commission, shall adopt European regulations or European decisions in order to implement the European laws referred to in the first paragraph.

The acts referred to in this Article shall include necessary provisions on legal safeguards.

SECTION 5

RULES ON COMPETITION

Subsection 1

Rules applying to undertakings

ARTICLE III-161

1. The following shall be prohibited as incompatible with the internal market: all agreements between undertakings, decisions by associations of undertakings and concerted practices which may affect trade between Member States and which have as their object or effect the prevention, restriction or distortion of competition within the internal market, and in particular those which:

(a) directly or indirectly fix purchase or selling prices or any other trading conditions;

(b) limit or control production, markets, technical development, or investment;

(c) share markets or sources of supply;

(d) apply dissimilar conditions to equivalent transactions with other trading parties, thereby placing them at a competitive disadvantage;

(e) make the conclusion of contracts subject to acceptance by the other parties of supplementary obligations which, by their nature or according to commercial usage, have no connection with the subject of such contracts.

2. Any agreements or decisions prohibited pursuant to this Article shall be automatically void.

3. Paragraph 1 may, however, be declared inapplicable in the case of:

–   any agreement or category of agreements between undertakings,

–   any decision or category of decisions by associations of undertakings,

–   any concerted practice or category of concerted practices,

which contributes to improving the production or distribution of goods or to promoting technical or economic progress, while allowing consumers a fair share of the resulting benefit, and which does not:

(a)   impose on the undertakings concerned restrictions which are not indispensable to the attainment of these objectives;

(b)   afford such undertakings the possibility of eliminating competition in respect of a substantial part of the products in question.

ARTICLE III-162

Any abuse by one or more undertakings of a dominant position within the internal market or in a substantial part of it shall be prohibited as incompatible with the internal market insofar as it may affect trade between Member States.

Such abuse may, in particular, consist in:

(a)   directly or indirectly imposing unfair purchase or selling prices or other unfair trading conditions;

(b)   limiting production, markets or technical development to the prejudice of consumers;

(c)   applying dissimilar conditions to equivalent transactions with other trading parties, thereby placing them at a competitive disadvantage;

(d)   making the conclusion of contracts subject to acceptance by the other parties of supplementary obligations which, by their nature or according to commercial usage, have no connection with the subject of such contracts.

ARTICLE III-163

The Council, on a proposal from the Commission, shall adopt the European regulations to give effect to the principles set out in Articles III-161 and III-162. It shall act after consulting the European Parliament.

Such regulations shall be designed in particular:

(a)   to ensure compliance with the prohibitions laid down in Article III-161(1) and in Article III-162 by making provision for fines and periodic penalty payments;

(b)   to lay down detailed rules for the application of Article III-161(3), taking into account the need to ensure effective supervision on the one hand, and to simplify administration to the greatest possible extent on the other;

(c)   to define, if need be, in the various branches of the economy, the scope of Articles III-161 and III-162;

(d)   to define the respective functions of the Commission and of the Court of Justice of the European Union in applying the provisions laid down in this paragraph;

(e)   to determine the relationship between Member States' laws and this Subsection as well as the European regulations adopted pursuant to this Article.

ARTICLE III-164

Until the entry into force of the European regulations adopted pursuant to Article III-163, the authorities in Member States shall rule on the admissibility of agreements, decisions and concerted practices and on abuse of a dominant position in the internal market in accordance with their national law and Article III-161, in particular paragraph 3, and Article III-162.

ARTICLE III-165

1.   Without prejudice to Article III-164, the Commission shall ensure the application of the principles set out in Articles III-161 and III-162. On application by a Member State or on its own initiative, and in cooperation with the competent authorities in the Member States, which shall give it their assistance, the Commission shall investigate cases of suspected infringement of these principles. If it finds that there has been an infringement, it shall propose appropriate measures to bring it to an end.

2.   If the infringement referred to in paragraph 1 is not brought to an end, the Commission shall adopt a reasoned European decision recording the infringement of the principles. The Commission may publish its decision and authorise Member States to take the measures, the conditions and details of which it shall determine, needed to remedy the situation.

3.   The Commission may adopt European regulations relating to the categories of agreement in respect of which the Council has adopted a European regulation pursuant to Article III-163, second paragraph, (b).

ARTICLE III-166

1.   In the case of public undertakings and undertakings to which Member States grant special or exclusive rights, Member States shall neither enact nor maintain in force any measure contrary to the Constitution, in particular Article I-4(2) and Articles III-161 to III-169.

2.   Undertakings entrusted with the operation of services of general economic interest or having the character of an income-producing monopoly shall be subject to the provisions of the Constitution, in particular to the rules on competition, insofar as the application of such provisions does not obstruct the performance, in law or in fact, of the particular tasks assigned to them. The development of trade must not be affected to such an extent as would be contrary to the Union's interests.

3.   The Commission shall ensure the application of this Article and shall, where necessary, adopt appropriate European regulations or decisions.

Subsection 2

Aids granted by Member States

ARTICLE III-167

1.   Save as otherwise provided in the Constitution, any aid granted by a Member State or through State resources in any form whatsoever which distorts or threatens to distort competition by favouring certain undertakings or the production of certain goods shall, insofar as it affects trade between Member States, be incompatible with the internal market.

2.   The following shall be compatible with the internal market:

(a)   aid having a social character, granted to individual consumers, provided that such aid is granted without discrimination related to the origin of the products concerned;

(b)   aid to make good the damage caused by natural disasters or exceptional occurrences;

(c)   aid granted to the economy of certain areas of the Federal Republic of Germany affected by the division of Germany, insofar as such aid is required in order to compensate for the economic disadvantages caused by that division. Five years after the entry into force of the Treaty establishing a Constitution for Europe, the Council, acting on a proposal from the Commission, may adopt a European decision repealing this point.

3.   The following may be considered to be compatible with the internal market:

(a)   aid to promote the economic development of areas where the standard of living is abnormally low or where there is serious underemployment, and of the regions referred to in Article III-424, in view of their structural, economic and social situation;

(b)   aid to promote the execution of an important project of common European interest or to remedy a serious disturbance in the economy of a Member State;

(c)   aid to facilitate the development of certain economic activities or of certain economic areas, where such aid does not adversely affect trading conditions to an extent contrary to the common interest;

(d)   aid to promote culture and heritage conservation where such aid does not affect trading conditions and competition in the Union to an extent that is contrary to the common interest;

(e)   such other categories of aid as may be specified by European regulations or decisions adopted by the Council on a proposal from the Commission.

ARTICLE III-168

1.   The Commission, in cooperation with Member States, shall keep under constant review all systems of aid existing in those States. It shall propose to the latter any appropriate measures required by the progressive development or by the functioning of the internal market.

2.   If, after giving notice to the parties concerned to submit their comments, the Commission finds that aid granted by a Member State or through State resources is not compatible with the internal market having regard to Article III-167, or that such aid is being misused, it shall adopt a European decision requiring the Member State concerned to abolish or alter such aid within a period of time to be determined by the Commission.

If the Member State concerned does not comply with this European decision within the prescribed time, the Commission or any other interested Member State may, in derogation from Articles III-360 and III-361, refer the matter to the Court of Justice of the European Union directly.

On application by a Member State, the Council may adopt unanimously a European decision that aid which that State is granting or intends to grant shall be considered to be compatible with the internal market, in derogation from Article III-167 or from European regulations provided for in Article III-169, if such a decision is justified by exceptional circumstances. If, as regards the aid in question, the Commission has already initiated the procedure provided for in the first subparagraph of this paragraph, the fact that the Member State concerned has made its application to the Council shall have the effect of suspending that procedure until the Council has made its attitude known.

If, however, the Council has not made its attitude known within three months of the said application being made, the Commission shall act.

3.   The Commission shall be informed by the Member States, in sufficient time to enable it to submit its comments, of any plans to grant or alter aid. If it considers that any such plan is not compatible with the internal market having regard to Article III-167, it shall without delay initiate the procedure provided for in paragraph 2 of this Article. The Member State concerned shall not put its proposed measures into effect until this procedure has resulted in a final decision.

4.   The Commission may adopt European regulations relating to the categories of State aid that the Council has, pursuant to Article III-169, determined may be exempted from the procedure provided for by paragraph 3 of this Article.

ARTICLE III-169

The Council, on a proposal from the Commission, may adopt European regulations for the application of Articles III-167 and III-168 and for determining in particular the conditions in which Article III-168(3) shall apply and the categories of aid exempted from the procedure provided for in Article 168(3). It shall act after consulting the European Parliament.

SECTION 6

FISCAL PROVISIONS

ARTICLE III-170

1.   No Member State shall impose, directly or indirectly, on the products of other Member States any internal taxation of any kind in excess of that imposed directly or indirectly on similar domestic products.

Furthermore, no Member State shall impose on the products of other Member States any internal taxation of such a nature as to afford indirect protection to other products.

2.   Where products are exported by a Member State to the territory of another Member State, any repayment of internal taxation shall not exceed the internal taxation imposed on them whether directly or indirectly.

3.   In the case of charges other than turnover taxes, excise duties and other forms of indirect taxation, remissions and repayments in respect of exports to other Member States may not be granted and countervailing charges in respect of imports from Member States may not be imposed unless the provisions contemplated have been previously approved for a limited period by a European decision adopted by the Council on a proposal from the Commission.

ARTICLE III-171

A European law or framework law of the Council shall establish measures for the harmonisation of legislation concerning turnover taxes, excise duties and other forms of indirect taxation provided that such harmonisation is necessary to ensure the establishment and the functioning of the internal market and to avoid distortion of competition. The Council shall act unanimously after consulting the European Parliament and the Economic and Social Committee.

SECTION 7

COMMON PROVISIONS

ARTICLE III-172

1.   Save where otherwise provided in the Constitution, this Article shall apply for the achievement of the objectives set out in Article III-130. European laws or framework laws shall establish measures for the approximation of the provisions laid down by law, regulation or administrative action in Member States which have as their object the establishment and functioning of the internal market. Such laws shall be adopted after consultation of the Economic and Social Committee.

2.   Paragraph 1 shall not apply to fiscal provisions, to those relating to the free movement of persons or to those relating to the rights and interests of employed persons.

3.   The Commission, in its proposals submitted under paragraph 1 concerning health, safety, environmental protection and consumer protection, shall take as a base a high level of protection, taking account in particular of any new development based on scientific facts. Within their respective powers, the European Parliament and the Council shall also seek to achieve this objective.

4.   If, after the adoption of a harmonisation measure by means of a European law or framework law or by means of a European regulation of the Commission, a Member State deems it necessary to maintain national provisions on grounds of major needs referred to in Article III-154, or relating to the protection of the environment or the working environment, it shall notify the Commission of these provisions as well as the grounds for maintaining them.

5.   Moreover, without prejudice to paragraph 4, if, after the adoption of a harmonisation measure by means of a European law or framework law or by means of a European regulation of the Commission, a Member State deems it necessary to introduce national provisions based on new scientific evidence relating to the protection of the environment or the working environment on grounds of a problem specific to that Member State arising after the adoption of the harmonisation measure, it shall notify the Commission of the envisaged provisions and the reasons for them.

6.   The Commission shall, within six months of the notifications referred to in paragraphs 4 and 5, adopt a European decision approving or rejecting the national provisions involved after having verified whether or not they are a means of arbitrary discrimination or a disguised restriction on trade between Member States and whether or not they constitute an obstacle to the functioning of the internal market.

In the absence of a decision by the Commission within this period the national provisions referred to in paragraphs 4 and 5 shall be deemed to have been approved.

When justified by the complexity of the matter and in the absence of danger to human health, the Commission may notify the Member State concerned that the period referred to in this paragraph will be extended for a further period of up to six months.

7.   When, pursuant to paragraph 6, a Member State is authorised to maintain or introduce national provisions derogating from a harmonisation measure, the Commission shall immediately examine whether to propose an adaptation to that measure.

8.   When a Member State raises a specific problem on public health in a field which has been the subject of prior harmonisation measures, it shall bring it to the attention of the Commission which shall immediately examine whether to propose appropriate measures.

9.   By way of derogation from the procedure laid down in Articles III-360 and III-361, the Commission and any Member State may bring the matter directly before the Court of Justice of the European Union if it considers that another Member State is making improper use of the powers provided for in this Article.

10.   The harmonisation measures referred to in this Article shall, in appropriate cases, include a safeguard clause authorising the Member States to take, for one or more of the non-economic reasons referred to in Article III-154, provisional measures subject to a Union control procedure.

ARTICLE III-173

Without prejudice to Article III-172, a European framework law of the Council shall establish measures for the approximation of such laws, regulations or administrative provisions of the Member States as directly affect the establishment or functioning of the internal market. The Council shall act unanimously after consulting the European Parliament and the Economic and Social Committee.

ARTICLE III-174

Where the Commission finds that a difference between the provisions laid down by law, regulation or administrative action in Member States is distorting the conditions of competition in the internal market and that the resultant distortion needs to be eliminated, it shall consult the Member States concerned.

If such consultation does not result in agreement, European framework laws shall establish the measures necessary to eliminate the distortion in question. Any other appropriate measures provided for in the Constitution may be adopted.

ARTICLE III-175

1.   Where there is reason to fear that the adoption or amendment of a provision laid down by law, regulation or administrative action of a Member State may cause distortion within the meaning of Article III-174, a Member State desiring to proceed therewith shall consult the Commission. After consulting the Member States, the Commission shall address to the Member States concerned a recommendation on such measures as may be appropriate to avoid the distortion in question.

2.   If a Member State desiring to introduce or amend its own provisions does not comply with the recommendation addressed to it by the Commission, other Member States shall not be required, pursuant to Article III-174, to amend their own provisions in order to eliminate such distortion. If the Member State which has ignored the recommendation of the Commission causes distortion detrimental only to itself, Article III-174 shall not apply.

ARTICLE III-176

In the context of the establishment and functioning of the internal market, European laws or framework laws shall establish measures for the creation of European intellectual property rights to provide uniform intellectual property rights protection throughout the Union and for the setting up of centralised Union-wide authorisation, coordination and supervision arrangements.

A European law of the Council shall establish language arrangements for the European intellectual property rights. The Council shall act unanimously after consulting the European Parliament.

CHAPTER II

ECONOMIC AND MONETARY POLICY

ARTICLE III-177

For the purposes set out in Article I-3, the activities of the Member States and the Union shall include, as provided in the Constitution, the adoption of an economic policy which is based on the close coordination of Member States' economic policies, on the internal market and on the definition of common objectives, and conducted in accordance with the principle of an open market economy with free competition.

Concurrently with the foregoing, and as provided in the Constitution and in accordance with the procedures set out therein, these activities shall include a single currency, the euro, and the definition and conduct of a single monetary policy and exchange-rate policy, the primary objective of both of which shall be to maintain price stability and, without prejudice to this objective, to support general economic policies in the Union, in accordance with the principle of an open market economy with free competition.

These activities of the Member States and the Union shall entail compliance with the following guiding principles: stable prices, sound public finances and monetary conditions and a stable balance of payments.

SECTION 1

ECONOMIC POLICY

ARTICLE III-178

Member States shall conduct their economic policies in order to contribute to the achievement of the Union's objectives, as defined in Article I-3, and in the context of the broad guidelines referred to in Article III-179(2). The Member States and the Union shall act in accordance with the principle of an open market economy with free competition, favouring an efficient allocation of resources, and in compliance with the principles set out in Article III-177.

ARTICLE III-179

1.   Member States shall regard their economic policies as a matter of common concern and shall coordinate them within the Council, in accordance with Article III-178.

2.   The Council, on a recommendation from the Commission, shall formulate a draft for the broad guidelines of the economic policies of the Member States and of the Union, and shall report its findings to the European Council.

The European Council, on the basis of the report from the Council, shall discuss a conclusion on the broad guidelines of the economic policies of the Member States and of the Union. On the basis of this conclusion, the Council shall adopt a recommendation setting out these broad guidelines. It shall inform the European Parliament of its recommendation.

3.   In order to ensure closer coordination of economic policies and sustained convergence of the economic performances of the Member States, the Council, on the basis of reports submitted by the Commission, shall monitor economic developments in each of the Member States and in the Union, as well as the consistency of economic policies with the broad guidelines referred to in paragraph 2, and shall regularly carry out an overall assessment.

For the purpose of this multilateral surveillance, Member States shall forward information to the Commission on important measures taken by them in the field of their economic policy and such other information as they deem necessary.

4.   Where it is established, under the procedure referred to in paragraph 3, that the economic policies of a Member State are not consistent with the broad guidelines referred to in paragraph 2 or that they risk jeopardising the proper functioning of economic and monetary union, the Commission may address a warning to the Member State concerned. The Council, on a recommendation from the Commission, may address the necessary recommendations to the Member State concerned. The Council, on a proposal from the Commission, may decide to make its recommendations public.

Within the scope of this paragraph, the Council shall act without taking into account the vote of the member of the Council representing the Member State concerned.

A qualified majority shall be defined as at least 55% of the other members of the Council, representing Member States comprising at least 65% of the population of the participating Member States.

A blocking minority must include at least the minimum number of these other Council members representing more than 35% of the population of the participating Member States, plus one member, failing which the qualified majority shall be deemed attained.

5.   The President of the Council and the Commission shall report to the European Parliament on the results of multilateral surveillance. The President of the Council may be invited to appear before the competent committee of the European Parliament if the Council has made its recommendations public.

6.   European laws may lay down detailed rules for the multilateral surveillance procedure referred to in paragraphs 3 and 4.

ARTICLE III-180

1.   Without prejudice to any other procedures provided for in the Constitution, the Council, on a proposal from the Commission, may adopt a European decision laying down measures appropriate to the economic situation, in particular if severe difficulties arise in the supply of certain products.

2.   Where a Member State is in difficulties or is seriously threatened with severe difficulties caused by natural disasters or exceptional occurrences beyond its control, the Council, on a proposal from the Commission, may adopt a European decision granting, under certain

conditions, Union financial assistance to the Member State concerned. The President of the Council shall inform the European Parliament of the decision adopted.

ARTICLE III-181

1.   Overdraft facilities or any other type of credit facility with the European Central Bank or with the central banks of the Member States (hereinafter referred to as "national central banks") in favour of Union institutions, bodies, offices or agencies, central governments, regional, local or other public authorities, other bodies governed by public law, or public undertakings of Member States shall be prohibited, as shall the purchase directly from them by the European Central Bank or national central banks of debt instruments.

2.   Paragraph 1 shall not apply to publicly owned credit institutions which, in the context of the supply of reserves by central banks, shall be given the same treatment by national central banks and the European Central Bank as private credit institutions.

ARTICLE III-182

Any measure or provision, not based on prudential considerations, establishing privileged access by Union institutions, bodies, offices or agencies, central governments, regional, local or other public authorities, other bodies governed by public law, or public undertakings of Member States · to financial institutions shall be prohibited.

ARTICLE III-183

1.   The Union shall not be liable for or assume the commitments of central governments, regional, local or other public authorities, other bodies governed by public law, or public undertakings of any Member State, without prejudice to mutual financial guarantees for the joint execution of a specific project. A Member State shall not be liable for or assume the commitments of central governments, regional, local or other public authorities, other bodies governed by public law, or public undertakings of another Member State, without prejudice to mutual financial guarantees for the joint execution of a specific project.

2.   The Council, on a proposal from the Commission, may adopt European regulations or decisions specifying definitions for the application of the prohibitions laid down in Articles III-181 and III-182 and in this Article. It shall act after consulting the European Parliament.

ARTICLE III-184

1.   Member States shall avoid excessive government deficits.

2.   The Commission shall monitor the development of the budgetary situation and of the stock of government debt in the Member States in order to identify gross errors. In particular it shall examine compliance with budgetary discipline on the basis of the following two criteria:

(a)   whether the ratio of the planned or actual government deficit to gross domestic product exceeds a reference value, unless:

   (i)   either the ratio has declined substantially and continuously and reached a level that comes close to the reference value, or

   (ii)   alternatively, the excess over the reference value is only exceptional and temporary and the ratio remains close to the reference value;

(b)   whether the ratio of government debt to gross domestic product exceeds a reference value, unless the ratio is diminishing sufficiently and approaching the reference value at a satisfactory pace.

The reference values are specified in the Protocol on the excessive deficit procedure.

3.   If a Member State does not fulfil the requirements under one or both of these criteria, the Commission shall prepare a report. The Commission's report shall also take into account whether the government deficit exceeds government investment expenditure and take into account all other relevant factors, including the medium-term economic and budgetary position of the Member State.

The Commission may also prepare a report if, notwithstanding the fulfilment of the requirements under the criteria, it is of the opinion that there is a risk of an excessive deficit in a Member State.

4.   The Economic and Financial Committee set up under Article III-192 shall formulate an opinion on the Commission's report.

5.   If the Commission considers that an excessive deficit in a Member State exists or may occur, it shall address an opinion to the Member State concerned and shall inform the Council accordingly.

6.   The Council shall, on a proposal from the Commission, having considered any observations which the Member State concerned may wish to make and after an overall assessment, decide whether an excessive deficit exists. In that case it shall adopt, without undue delay, on a recommendation from the Commission, recommendations addressed to the Member State concerned with a view to bringing that situation to an end within a given period. Subject to paragraph 8, those recommendations shall not be made public.

Within the scope of this paragraph, the Council shall act without taking into account the vote of the member of the Council representing the Member State concerned.

A qualified majority shall be defined as at least 55% of the other members of the Council, representing Member States comprising at least 65% of the population of the participating Member States.

A blocking minority must include at least the minimum number of these other Council members representing more than 35% of the population of the participating Member States, plus one member, failing which the qualified majority shall be deemed attained.

7.   The Council, on a recommendation from the Commission, shall adopt the European decisions and recommendations referred to in paragraphs 8 to 11.

It shall act without taking into account the vote of the member of the Council representing the Member State concerned.

A qualified majority shall be defined as at least 55% of the other members of the Council, representing Member States comprising at least 65% of the population of the participating Member States.

A blocking minority must include at least the minimum number of these other Council members representing more than 35% of the population of the participating Member States, plus one member, failing which the qualified majority shall be deemed attained.

8.   Where it adopts a European decision establishing that there has been no effective action in response to its recommendations within the period laid down, the Council may make its recommendations public.

9.   If a Member State persists in failing to put the Council's recommendations into practice, the Council may adopt a European decision giving notice to the Member State to take, within a specified time-limit, measures for the deficit reduction which the Council judges necessary to remedy the situation.

In such a case, the Council may request the Member State concerned to submit reports in accordance with a specific timetable in order to examine the adjustment efforts of that Member State.

10.   As long as a Member State fails to comply with a European decision adopted in accordance with paragraph 9, the Council may decide to apply or, as the case may be, intensify one or more of the following measures:

(a)   require the Member State concerned to publish additional information, to be specified by the Council, before issuing bonds and securities;

(b)   invite the European Investment Bank to reconsider its lending policy towards the Member State concerned;

(c)   require the Member State concerned to make a non-interest-bearing deposit of an appropriate size with the Union until the Council considers that the excessive deficit has been corrected;

(d)   impose fines of an appropriate size.

The President of the Council shall inform the European Parliament of the measures adopted.

11.   The Council shall repeal some or all of the measures referred to in paragraph 6 and paragraphs 8, 9 and 10 if it considers the excessive deficit in the Member State concerned to have been corrected. If the Council has previously made public recommendations, it shall state publicly, as soon as the European decision referred to in paragraph 8 has been repealed, that there is no longer an excessive deficit in the Member State concerned.

12.   The rights to bring actions provided for in Articles III-360 and III-361 shall not be exercised within the framework of paragraphs 1 to 6 or paragraphs 8 and 9.

13.   Further provisions relating to the implementation of the procedure laid down in this Article are set out in the Protocol on the excessive deficit procedure.

A European law of the Council shall lay down the appropriate measures to replace the said Protocol. The Council shall act unanimously after consulting the European Parliament and the European Central Bank.

Subject to the other provisions of this paragraph, the Council, on a proposal from the Commission, shall adopt European regulations or decisions laying down detailed rules and definitions for the application of the said Protocol. It shall act after consulting the European Parliament.

SECTION 2

MONETARY POLICY

ARTICLE III-185

1.   The primary objective of the European System of Central Banks shall be to maintain price stability. Without prejudice to this objective, the European System of Central Banks shall support the general economic policies in the Union in order to contribute to the achievement of its objectives as laid down in Article I-3. The European System of Central Banks shall act in accordance with the principle of an open market economy with free competition, favouring an efficient allocation of resources, and in compliance with the principles set out in Article III-177.

2.   The basic tasks to be carried out through the European System of Central Banks shall be:

(a)   to define and implement the Union's monetary policy;

(b)   to conduct foreign-exchange operations consistent with Article III-326;

(c)   to hold and manage the official foreign reserves of the Member States;

(d)   to promote the smooth operation of payment systems.

3.   Paragraph 2(c) shall be without prejudice to the holding and management by the governments of Member States of foreign-exchange working balances.

4.   The European Central Bank shall be consulted:

(a)   on any proposed Union act in areas within its powers;

(b)   by national authorities regarding any draft legislative provision in areas within its powers, but within the limits and under the conditions set out by the Council in accordance with the procedure laid down in Article III-187(4).

The European Central Bank may submit opinions to the Union institutions, bodies, offices or agencies or to national authorities on matters within its powers.

5.   The European System of Central Banks shall contribute to the smooth conduct of policies pursued by the competent authorities relating to the prudential supervision of credit institutions and the stability of the financial system.

6.   A European law of the Council may confer specific tasks upon the European Central Bank concerning policies relating to the prudential supervision of credit institutions and other

financial institutions with the exception of insurance undertakings. The Council shall act unanimously after consulting the European Parliament and the European Central Bank.

ARTICLE III-186

1.   The European Central Bank shall have the exclusive right to authorise the issue of euro bank notes in the Union. The European Central Bank and the national central banks may issue such notes. Only the bank notes issued by the European Central Bank and the national central banks shall have the status of legal tender within the Union.

2.   Member States may issue euro coins subject to approval by the European Central Bank of the volume of the issue.

The Council, on a proposal from the Commission, may adopt European regulations laying down measures to harmonise the denominations and technical specifications of coins intended for circulation to the extent necessary to permit their smooth circulation within the Union. The Council shall act after consulting the European Parliament and the European Central Bank.

ARTICLE III-187

1.   The European System of Central Banks shall be governed by the decision-making bodies of the European Central Bank, which shall be the Governing Council and the Executive Board.

2.   The Statute of the European System of Central Banks is laid down in the Protocol on the Statute of the European System of Central Banks and of the European Central Bank.

3.   Article 5(1), (2) and (3), Articles 17 and 18, Article 19(1), Articles 22, 23, 24 and 26, Article 32(2), (3), (4) and (6), Article 33(1)(a) and Article 36 of the Statute of the European System of Central Banks and of the European Central Bank may be amended by European laws:

(a)   either on a proposal from the Commission and after consultation of the European Central Bank;

(b)   or on a recommendation from the European Central Bank and after consultation of the Commission.

4.   The Council shall adopt the European regulations and decisions laying down the measures referred to in Article 4, Article 5(4), Article 19(2), Article 20, Article 28(1), Article 29(2), Article 30(4) and Article 34(3) of the Statute of the European System of Central Banks and of the European Central Bank. It shall act after consulting the European Parliament:

(a)   either on a proposal from the Commission and after consulting the European Central Bank;

(b)   or on a recommendation from the European Central Bank and after consulting the Commission.

ARTICLE III-188

When exercising the powers and carrying out the tasks and duties conferred upon them by the Constitution and the Statute of the European System of Central Banks and of the European Central Bank, neither the European Central Bank, nor a national central bank, nor any member of their decision-making bodies shall seek or take instructions from Union institutions, bodies, offices or agencies, from any government of a Member State or from any other body. The Union institutions, bodies, offices or agencies and the governments of the Member States undertake to respect this principle and not to seek to influence the members of the decision-making bodies of the European Central Bank or of the national central banks in the performance of their tasks.

ARTICLE III-189

Each Member State shall ensure that its national legislation, including the statutes of its national central bank, is compatible with the Constitution and the Statute of the European System of Central Banks and of the European Central Bank.

ARTICLE III-190

1.   In order to carry out the tasks entrusted to the European System of Central Banks, the European Central Bank shall, in accordance with the Constitution and under the conditions laid down in the Statute of the European System of Central Banks and of the European Central Bank, adopt:

(a)   European regulations to the extent necessary to implement the tasks defined in Article 3(1)(a), Article 19(1), Article 22 and Article 25(2) of the Statute of the European System of Central Banks and of the European Central Bank and in cases which shall be laid down in European regulations and decisions as referred to in Article III-187(4);

(b)   European decisions necessary for carrying out the tasks entrusted to the European System of Central Banks under the Constitution and the Statute of the European System of Central Banks and of the European Central Bank;

(c)   recommendations and opinions.

2.   The European Central Bank may decide to publish its European decisions, recommendations and opinions.

3.   The Council shall, under the procedure laid down in Article III-187(4), adopt the European regulations establishing the limits and conditions under which the European Central Bank shall be entitled to impose fines or periodic penalty payments on undertakings for failure to comply with obligations under its European regulations and decisions.

ARTICLE III-191

Without prejudice to the powers of the European Central Bank, European laws or framework laws shall lay down the measures necessary for use of the euro as the single currency. Such laws or framework laws shall be adopted after consultation of the European Central Bank.

SECTION 3

INSTITUTIONAL PROVISIONS

ARTICLE III-192

1.   In order to promote coordination of the policies of Member States to the full extent needed for the functioning of the internal market, an Economic and Financial Committee is hereby set up.

2.   The Committee shall have the following tasks:

(a)   to deliver opinions at the request of the Council or of the Commission, or on its own initiative, for submission to those institutions;

(b)   to keep under review the economic and financial situation of the Member States and of the Union and to report on it regularly to the Council and to the Commission, in particular with regard to financial relations with third countries and international institutions;

(c)   without prejudice to Article III-344, to contribute to the preparation of the work of the Council referred to in Article III-159, Article III-179(2), (3), (4) and (6), Articles III-180, III-183 and III-184, Article III-185(6), Article III-186(2), Article III-187(3) and (4), Articles III-191 and III-196, Article III-198(2) and (3), Article III-201, Article III-202(2) and (3) and Articles III-322 and III-326, and to carry out other advisory and preparatory tasks assigned to it by the Council;

(d)   to examine, at least once a year, the situation regarding the movement of capital and the freedom of payments, as they result from the application of the Constitution and of Union acts; the examination shall cover all measures relating to capital movements and payments; the Committee shall report to the Commission and to the Council on the outcome of this examination.

The Member States, the Commission and the European Central Bank shall each appoint no more than two members of the Committee.

3.   The Council, on a proposal from the Commission, shall adopt a European decision laying down detailed provisions concerning the composition of the Economic and Financial Committee. It shall act after consulting the European Central Bank and the Committee. The President of the Council shall inform the European Parliament of that decision.

4.   In addition to the tasks referred to in paragraph 2, if and as long as there are Member States with a derogation as referred to in Article III-197, the Committee shall keep under review the monetary and financial situation and the general payments system of those Member States and report regularly to the Council and to the Commission on the matter.

ARTICLE III-193

For matters within the scope of Article III-179(4), Article III-184 with the exception of paragraph 13, Articles III-191, III-196, Article III-198(3) and Article III-326, the Council or a Member State may request the Commission to make a recommendation or a proposal, as appropriate. The Commission shall examine this request and submit its conclusions to the Council without delay.

SECTION 4

PROVISIONS SPECIFIC TO MEMBER STATES WHOSE CURRENCY IS THE EURO

ARTICLE III-194

1.   In order to ensure the proper functioning of economic and monetary union, and in accordance with the relevant provisions of the Constitution, the Council shall, in accordance with the relevant procedure from among those referred to in Articles III-179 and III-184, with the exception of the procedure set out in Article III-184(13), adopt measures specific to those Member States whose currency is the euro:

(a)   to strengthen the coordination and surveillance of their budgetary discipline;

(b)   to set out economic policy guidelines for them, while ensuring that they are compatible with those adopted for the whole of the Union and are kept under surveillance.

2.   For those measures set out in paragraph 1, only members of the Council representing Member States whose currency is the euro shall take part in the vote.

A qualified majority shall be defined as at least 55% of these members of the Council, representing Member States comprising at least 65% of the population of the participating Member States.

A blocking minority must include at least the minimum number of these Council members representing more than 35% of the population of the participating Member States, plus one member, failing which the qualified majority shall be deemed attained.

ARTICLE III-195

Arrangements for meetings between ministers of those Member States whose currency is the euro are laid down by the Protocol on the Euro Group.

ARTICLE III-196

1.   In order to secure the euro's place in the international monetary system, the Council, on a proposal from the Commission, shall adopt a European decision establishing common positions on matters of particular interest for economic and monetary union within the competent international financial institutions and conferences. The Council shall act after consulting the European Central Bank.

2.   The Council, on a proposal from the Commission, may adopt appropriate measures to ensure unified representation within the international financial institutions and conferences. The Council shall act after consulting the European Central Bank.

3.   For the measures referred to in paragraphs 1 and 2, only members of the Council representing Member States whose currency is the euro shall take part in the vote.

A qualified majority shall be defined as at least 55% of these members of the Council, representing Member States comprising at least 65% of the population of the participating Member States.

A blocking minority must include at least the minimum number of these Council members representing more than 35% of the population of the participating Member States, plus one member, failing which the qualified majority shall be deemed attained.

SECTION 5

TRANSITIONAL PROVISIONS

ARTICLE III-197

1.   Member States in respect of which the Council has not decided that they fulfil the necessary conditions for the adoption of the euro shall hereinafter be referred to as "Member States with a derogation".

2.   The following provisions of the Constitution shall not apply to Member States with a derogation:

(a)   adoption of the parts of the broad economic policy guidelines which concern the euro area generally (Article III-179(2));

(b)   coercive means of remedying excessive deficits (Article III-184(9) and (10));

(c)   the objectives and tasks of the European System of Central Banks (Article III-185(1), (2), (3) and (5));

(d)   issue of the euro (Article III-186);

(e)   acts of the European Central Bank (Article III-190);

(f)   measures governing the use of the euro (Article III-191);

(g)   monetary agreements and other measures relating to exchange-rate policy (Article III-326);

(h)   appointment of members of the Executive Board of the European Central Bank (Article III-382(2));

(i)   European decisions establishing common positions on issues of particular relevance for economic and monetary union within the competent international financial institutions and conferences (Article III-196(1));

(j)   measures to ensure unified representation within the international financial institutions and conferences (Article III-196(2)).

In the Articles referred to in points (a) to (j), "Member States" shall therefore mean Member States whose currency is the euro.

3.   Under Chapter IX of the Statute of the European System of Central Banks and of the European Central Bank, Member States with a derogation and their national central banks are excluded from rights and obligations within the European System of Central Banks.

4.   The voting rights of members of the Council representing Member States with a derogation shall be suspended for the adoption by the Council of the measures referred to in the Articles listed in paragraph 2, and in the following instances:

(a)   recommendations made to those Member States whose currency is the euro in the framework of multilateral surveillance, including on stability programmes and warnings (Article III-179(4));

(b)   measures relating to excessive deficits concerning those Member States whose currency is the euro (Article III-184(6), (7), (8) and (11)).

A qualified majority shall be defined as at least 55% of the other members of the Council, representing Member States comprising at least 65% of the population of the participating Member States.

A blocking minority must include at least the minimum number of these other Council members representing more than 35% of the population of the participating Member States, plus one member, failing which the qualified majority shall be deemed attained.

ARTICLE III-198

1.   At least once every two years, or at the request of a Member State with a derogation, the Commission and the European Central Bank shall report to the Council on the progress made by the Member States with a derogation in fulfilling their obligations regarding the achievement of economic and monetary union. These reports shall include an examination of the compatibility between the national legislation of each of these Member States, including the statutes of its national central bank, and Articles III-188 and III-189 and the Statute of the European System of Central Banks and of the European Central Bank. The reports shall also examine whether a high degree of sustainable convergence has been achieved, by analysing how far each of these Member States has fulfilled the following criteria:

(a)   the achievement of a high degree of price stability; this is apparent from a rate of inflation which is close to that of, at most, the three best performing Member States in terms of price stability;

(b)   the sustainability of the government financial position; this is apparent from having achieved a government budgetary position without a deficit that is excessive as determined in accordance with Article III-184(6);

(c)   the observance of the normal fluctuation margins provided for by the exchange-rate mechanism of the European monetary system, for at least two years, without devaluing against the euro;

(d)   the durability of convergence achieved by the Member State with a derogation and of its participation in the exchange-rate mechanism, being reflected in the long-term interest-rate levels.

The four criteria laid down in this paragraph and the relevant periods over which they are to be respected are developed further in the Protocol on the convergence criteria. The reports from the Commission and the European Central Bank shall also take account of the results of the integration of markets, the situation and development of the balances of payments on current account and an examination of the development of unit labour costs and other price indices.

2.   After consulting the European Parliament and after discussion in the European Council, the Council, on a proposal from the Commission, shall adopt a European decision establishing which Member States with a derogation fulfil the necessary conditions on the basis of the criteria laid down in paragraph 1, and shall abrogate the derogations of the Member States concerned.

The Council shall act having received a recommendation of a qualified majority of those among its members representing Member States whose currency is the euro. These members shall act within six months of the Council receiving the Commission's proposal.

The qualified majority referred to in the second subparagraph shall be defined as at least 55% of these members of the Council, representing Member States comprising at least 65% of the population of the participating Member States. A blocking minority must include at least the minimum number of these Council members representing more than 35% of the population of the participating Member States, plus one member, failing which the qualified majority shall be deemed attained.

3.   If it is decided, in accordance with the procedure set out in paragraph 2, to abrogate a derogation, the Council shall, on a proposal from the Commission, adopt the European regulations or decisions irrevocably fixing the rate at which the euro is to be substituted for the currency of the Member State concerned, and laying down the other measures necessary for the introduction of the euro as the single currency in that Member State. The Council shall act with the unanimous agreement of the members representing Member States whose currency is the euro and the Member State concerned, after consulting the European Central Bank.

ARTICLE III-199

1.   If and as long as there are Member States with a derogation, and without prejudice to Article III-187(1), the General Council of the European Central Bank referred to in Article 45 of the Statute of the European System of Central Banks and of the European Central Bank shall be constituted as a third decision-making body of the European Central Bank.

2.   If and as long as there are Member States with a derogation, the European Central Bank shall, as regards those Member States:

(a)   strengthen cooperation between the national central banks;

(b)   strengthen the coordination of the monetary policies of the Member States, with the aim of ensuring price stability;

(c)   monitor the functioning of the exchange-rate mechanism;

(d)   hold consultations concerning issues falling within the competence of the national central banks and affecting the stability of financial institutions and markets;

(e)   carry out the former tasks of the European Monetary Cooperation Fund which had subsequently been taken over by the European Monetary Institute.

ARTICLE III-200

Each Member State with a derogation shall treat its exchange-rate policy as a matter of common interest. In so doing, it shall take account of the experience acquired in cooperation within the framework of the exchange-rate mechanism.

ARTICLE III-201

1.   Where a Member State with a derogation is in difficulties or is seriously threatened with difficulties as regards its balance of payments either as a result of an overall disequilibrium in its balance of payments, or as a result of the type of currency at its disposal, and where such difficulties are liable in particular to jeopardise the functioning of the internal market or the implementation of the common commercial policy, the Commission shall immediately investigate the position of the State in question and the action which, making use of all the means at its disposal, that State has taken or may take in accordance with the Constitution. The Commission shall state what measures it recommends the Member State concerned to adopt.

If the action taken by a Member State with a derogation and the measures suggested by the Commission do not prove sufficient to overcome the difficulties which have arisen or which threaten, the Commission shall, after consulting the Economic and Financial Committee, recommend to the Council the granting of mutual assistance and appropriate methods.

The Commission shall keep the Council regularly informed of the situation and of how it evolves.

2.   The Council shall adopt European regulations or decisions granting such mutual assistance and laying down the conditions and details of such assistance, which may take such forms as:

(a)   a concerted approach to or within any other international organisations to which Member States with a derogation may have recourse;

(b)   measures needed to avoid deflection of trade where the Member State with a derogation, which is in difficulties, maintains or reintroduces quantitative restrictions against third countries;

(c)   the granting of limited credits by other Member States, subject to their agreement.

3.   If the mutual assistance recommended by the Commission is not granted by the Council or if the mutual assistance granted and the measures taken are insufficient, the Commission shall authorise the Member State with a derogation, which is in difficulties, to take protective measures, the conditions and details of which the Commission shall determine.

Such authorisation may be revoked and such conditions and details may be changed by the Council.

ARTICLE III-202

1.   Where a sudden crisis in the balance of payments occurs and a European decision as referred to in Article III-201(2) is not immediately adopted, a Member State with a derogation may, as a precaution, take the necessary protective measures. Such measures must cause the least possible disturbance in the functioning of the internal market and must not be wider in scope than is strictly necessary to remedy the sudden difficulties which have arisen.

2.   The Commission and the other Member States shall be informed of the protective measures referred to in paragraph 1 not later than when they enter into force. The Commission may recommend to the Council the granting of mutual assistance under Article III-201.

3.   The Council, acting on a recommendation from the Commission and after consulting the Economic and Financial Committee may adopt a European decision stipulating that the Member State concerned shall amend, suspend or abolish the protective measures referred to in paragraph 1.

CHAPTER III

POLICIES IN OTHER AREAS

SECTION 1

EMPLOYMENT

ARTICLE III-203

The Union and the Member States shall, in accordance with this Section, work towards developing a coordinated strategy for employment and particularly for promoting a skilled, trained and adaptable workforce and labour markets responsive to economic change with a view to achieving the objectives referred to in Article I-3.

ARTICLE III-204

1.   Member States, through their employment policies, shall contribute to the achievement of the objectives referred to in Article III-203 in a way consistent with the broad guidelines of the economic policies of the Member States and of the Union adopted pursuant to Article III-179(2).

2.   Member States, having regard to national practices related to the responsibilities of management and labour, shall regard promoting employment as a matter of common concern and shall coordinate their action in this respect within the Council, in accordance with Article III-206.

ARTICLE III-205

1.   The Union shall contribute to a high level of employment by encouraging cooperation between Member States and by supporting and, if necessary, complementing their action. In doing so, the competences of the Member States shall be respected.

2.   The objective of a high level of employment shall be taken into consideration in the formulation and implementation of Union policies and activities.

ARTICLE III-206

1.   The European Council shall each year consider the employment situation in the Union and adopt conclusions thereon, on the basis of a joint annual report by the Council and the Commission.

2.   On the basis of the conclusions of the European Council, the Council, on a proposal from the Commission, shall each year adopt guidelines which the Member States shall take into account in their employment policies. It shall act after consulting the European Parliament, the Committee of the Regions, the Economic and Social Committee and the Employment Committee.

These guidelines shall be consistent with the broad guidelines adopted pursuant to Article III-179(2).

3.   Each Member State shall provide the Council and the Commission with an annual report on the principal measures taken to implement its employment policy in the light of the guidelines for employment as referred to in paragraph 2.

4.   The Council, on the basis of the reports referred to in paragraph 3 and having received the views of the Employment Committee, shall each year carry out an examination of the implementation of the employment policies of the Member States in the light of the guidelines for employment. The Council, on a recommendation from the Commission, may adopt recommendations which it shall address to Member States.

5.   On the basis of the results of that examination, the Council and the Commission shall make a joint annual report to the European Council on the employment situation in the Union and on the implementation of the guidelines for employment.

ARTICLE III-207

European laws or framework laws may establish incentive measures designed to encourage cooperation between Member States and to support their action in the field of employment through initiatives aimed at developing exchanges of information and best practices, providing comparative analysis and advice as well as promoting innovative approaches and evaluating experiences, in particular by recourse to pilot projects. They shall be adopted after consultation of the Committee of the Regions and the Economic and Social Committee.

Such European laws or framework laws shall not include harmonisation of the laws and regulations of the Member States.

ARTICLE III-208

The Council shall, by a simple majority, adopt a European decision establishing an Employment Committee with advisory status to promote coordination between Member States on employment and labour market policies. It shall act after consulting the European Parliament.

The tasks of the Committee shall be:

(a)   to monitor the employment situation and employment policies in the Union and the Member States;

(b)   without prejudice to Article III-344, to formulate opinions at the request of either the Council or the Commission or on its own initiative, and to contribute to the preparation of the Council proceedings referred to in Article III-206.

In fulfilling its mandate, the Committee shall consult management and labour.

Each Member State and the Commission shall appoint two members of the Committee.

SECTION 2

SOCIAL POLICY

ARTICLE III-209

The Union and the Member States, having in mind fundamental social rights such as those set out in the European Social Charter signed at Turin on 18 October 1961 and in the 1989 Community Charter of the Fundamental Social Rights of Workers, shall have as their objectives the promotion of employment, improved living and working conditions, so as to make possible their harmonisation while the improvement is being maintained, proper social protection, dialogue between management and labour, the development of human resources with a view to lasting high employment and the combating of exclusion.

To this end the Union and the Member States shall act taking account of the diverse forms of national practices, in particular in the field of contractual relations, and the need to maintain the competitiveness of the Union economy.

They believe that such a development will ensue not only from the functioning of the internal market, which will favour the harmonisation of social systems, but also from the procedures provided for in the Constitution and from the approximation of provisions laid down by law, regulation or administrative action of the Member States.

ARTICLE III-210

1.   With a view to achieving the objectives of Article III-209, the Union shall support and complement the activities of the Member States in the following fields:

(a)   improvement in particular of the working environment to protect workers' health and safety;

(b)   working conditions;

(c)   social security and social protection of workers;

(d)   protection of workers where their employment contract is terminated;

(e)   the information and consultation of workers;

(f)   representation and collective defence of the interests of workers and employers, including co-determination, subject to paragraph 6;

(g)   conditions of employment for third-country nationals legally residing in Union territory;

(h)   the integration of persons excluded from the labour market, without prejudice to Article III-283;

(i)   equality between women and men with regard to labour market opportunities and treatment at work;

(j)   the combating of social exclusion;

(k)   the modernisation of social protection systems without prejudice to point (c).

2.   For the purposes of paragraph 1:

(a)   European laws or framework laws may establish measures designed to encourage cooperation between Member States through initiatives aimed at improving knowledge, developing exchanges of information and best practices, promoting innovative approaches and evaluating experiences, excluding any harmonisation of the laws and regulations of the Member States;

(b)   in the fields referred to in paragraph 1(a) to (i), European framework laws may establish minimum requirements for gradual implementation, having regard to the conditions and technical rules obtaining in each of the Member States. Such European framework laws shall avoid imposing administrative, financial and legal constraints in a way which would hold back the creation and development of small and medium-sized undertakings.

In all cases, such European laws or framework laws shall be adopted after consultation of the Committee of the Regions and the Economic and Social Committee.

3.   By way of derogation from paragraph 2, in the fields referred to in paragraph 1(c), (d), (f) and (g), European laws or framework laws shall be adopted by the Council acting unanimously after consulting the European Parliament, the Committee of the Regions and the Economic and Social Committee.

The Council may, on a proposal from the Commission, adopt a European decision making the ordinary legislative procedure applicable to paragraph 1(d), (f) and (g). It shall act unanimously after consulting the European Parliament.

4.   A Member State may entrust management and labour, at their joint request, with the implementation of European framework laws adopted pursuant to paragraphs 2 and 3 or, where appropriate, with the implementation of European regulations or decisions adopted in accordance with Article III-212.

In this case, it shall ensure that, no later than the date on which a European framework law must be transposed, or a European regulation or decision implemented, management and labour have introduced the necessary measures by agreement, the Member State concerned being required to take any necessary measure enabling it at any time to be in a position to guarantee the results imposed by that framework law, regulation or decision.

5.   The European laws and framework laws adopted pursuant to this Article:

(a)   shall not affect the right of Member States to define the fundamental principles of their social security systems and must not significantly affect the financial equilibrium of such systems;

(b)   shall not prevent any Member State from maintaining or introducing more stringent protective measures compatible with the Constitution.

6.   This Article shall not apply to pay, the right of association, the right to strike or the right to impose lock-outs.

ARTICLE III-211

1.   The Commission shall promote the consultation of management and labour at Union level and shall adopt any relevant measure to facilitate their dialogue by ensuring balanced support for the parties.

2.   For the purposes of paragraph 1, before submitting proposals in the social policy field, the Commission shall consult management and labour on the possible direction of Union action.

3.   If, after the consultation referred to in paragraph 2, the Commission considers Union action desirable, it shall consult management and labour on the content of the envisaged proposal. Management and labour shall forward to the Commission an opinion or, where appropriate, a recommendation.

4.   On the occasion of the consultation referred to in paragraphs 2 and 3, management and labour may inform the Commission of their wish to initiate the process provided for in Article III-212(1). The duration of this process shall not exceed nine months, unless the management and labour concerned and the Commission decide jointly to extend it.

ARTICLE III-212

1.   Should management and labour so desire, the dialogue between them at Union level may lead to contractual relations, including agreements.

2.   Agreements concluded at Union level shall be implemented either in accordance with the procedures and practices specific to management and labour and the Member States or, in matters covered by Article III-210, at the joint request of the signatory parties, by European regulations or decisions adopted by the Council on a proposal from the Commission. The European Parliament shall be informed.

Where the agreement in question contains one or more provisions relating to one of the areas for which unanimity is required pursuant to Article III-210(3), the Council shall act unanimously.

ARTICLE III-213

With a view to achieving the objectives of Article III-209 and without prejudice to the other provisions of the Constitution, the Commission shall encourage cooperation between the Member States and facilitate the coordination of their action in all social policy fields under this Section, particularly in matters relating to:

(a)   employment;

(b)   labour law and working conditions;

(c)   basic and advanced vocational training;

(d)   social security;

(e)   prevention of occupational accidents and diseases;

(f)   occupational hygiene;

(g)   the right of association and collective bargaining between employers and workers.

To this end, the Commission shall act in close contact with Member States by making studies, delivering opinions and arranging consultations both on problems arising at national level and on those of concern to international organisations, in particular initiatives aiming at the establishment of guidelines and indicators, the organisation of exchange of best practice, and the preparation of the necessary elements for periodic monitoring and evaluation. The European Parliament shall be kept fully informed.

Before delivering the opinions provided for in this Article, the Commission shall consult the Economic and Social Committee.

ARTICLE III-214

1.   Each Member State shall ensure that the principle of equal pay for female and male workers for equal work or work of equal value is applied.

2.   For the purpose of this Article, "pay" means the ordinary basic or minimum wage or salary and any other consideration, whether in cash or in kind, which the worker receives directly or indirectly, in respect of his employment, from his employer.

Equal pay without discrimination based on sex means:

(a)   that pay for the same work at piece rates shall be calculated on the basis of the same unit of measurement;

(b)   that pay for work at time rates shall be the same for the same job.

3.   European laws or framework laws shall establish measures to ensure the application of the principle of equal opportunities and equal treatment of women and men in matters of

employment and occupation, including the principle of equal pay for equal work or work of equal value. They shall be adopted after consultation of the Economic and Social Committee.

4.   With a view to ensuring full equality in practice between women and men in working life, the principle of equal treatment shall not prevent any Member State from maintaining or adopting measures providing for specific advantages in order to make it easier for the under-represented sex to pursue a vocational activity, or to prevent or compensate for disadvantages in professional careers.

ARTICLE III-215

Member States shall endeavour to maintain the existing equivalence between paid holiday schemes.

ARTICLE III-216

The Commission shall draw up a report each year on progress in achieving the objectives of Article III-209, including the demographic situation within the Union. It shall forward the report to the European Parliament, the Council and the Economic and Social Committee.

ARTICLE III-217

The Council shall, by a simple majority, adopt a European decision establishing a Social Protection Committee with advisory status to promote cooperation on social protection policies between Member States and with the Commission. The Council shall act after consulting the European Parliament.

The tasks of the Committee shall be:

(a)   to monitor the social situation and the development of social protection policies in the Member States and within the Union;

(b)   to promote exchanges of information, experience and good practice between Member States and with the Commission;

(c)   without prejudice to Article III-344, to prepare reports, formulate opinions or undertake other work within the scope of its powers, at the request of either the Council or the Commission or on its own initiative.

In fulfilling its mandate, the Committee shall establish appropriate contacts with management and labour.

Each Member State and the Commission shall appoint two members of the Committee.

ARTICLE III-218

The Commission shall include a separate chapter on social developments within the Union in its annual report to the European Parliament.

The European Parliament may invite the Commission to draw up reports on any particular problems concerning social conditions.

ARTICLE III-219

1. In order to improve employment opportunities for workers in the internal market and to contribute thereby to raising the standard of living, a European Social Fund is hereby established; it shall aim to render the employment of workers easier and to increase their geographical and occupational mobility within the Union, and to facilitate their adaptation to industrial changes and to changes in production systems, in particular through vocational training and retraining.

2. The Commission shall administer the Fund. It shall be assisted in this task by a Committee presided over by a member of the Commission and composed of representatives of Member States, trade unions and employers' organisations.

3. European laws shall establish implementing measures relating to the Fund. Such laws shall be adopted after consultation of the Committee of the Regions and the Economic and Social Committee.

SECTION 3

ECONOMIC, SOCIAL AND TERRITORIAL COHESION

ARTICLE III-220

In order to promote its overall harmonious development, the Union shall develop and pursue its action leading to the strengthening of its economic, social and territorial cohesion.

In particular, the Union shall aim at reducing disparities between the levels of development of the various regions and the backwardness of the least favoured regions.

Among the regions concerned, particular attention shall be paid to rural areas, areas affected by industrial transition, and regions which suffer from severe and permanent natural or demographic handicaps such as the northernmost regions with very low population density and island, cross-border and mountain regions.

ARTICLE III-221

Member States shall conduct their economic policies and shall coordinate them in such a way as, in addition, to attain the objectives set out in Article III-220. The formulation and implementation of the Union's policies and action and the implementation of the internal market shall take into account those objectives and shall contribute to their achievement. The Union shall also support the achievement of these objectives by the action it takes through the Structural Funds (European Agricultural Guidance and Guarantee Fund, Guidance Section; European Social Fund; European Regional Development Fund), the European Investment Bank and the other existing financial instruments.

The Commission shall submit a report to the European Parliament, the Council, the Committee of the Regions and the Economic and Social Committee every three years on the progress made towards achieving economic, social and territorial cohesion and on the manner in which the various means provided for in this Article have contributed to it. This report shall, if necessary, be accompanied by appropriate proposals.

European laws or framework laws may establish any specific measure outside the Funds, without prejudice to measures adopted within the framework of the Union's other policies. They shall be adopted after consultation of the Committee of the Regions and the Economic and Social Committee.

ARTICLE III-222

The European Regional Development Fund is intended to help to redress the main regional imbalances in the Union through participation in the development and structural adjustment of regions whose development is lagging behind and in the conversion of declining industrial regions.

ARTICLE III-223

1.   Without prejudice to Article III-224, European laws shall define the tasks, the priority objectives and the organisation of the Structural Funds, which may involve grouping the Funds, the general rules applicable to them and the provisions necessary to ensure their effectiveness and the coordination of the Funds with one another and with the other existing financial instruments.

A Cohesion Fund set up by a European law shall provide a financial contribution to projects in the fields of environment and trans-European networks in the area of transport infrastructure.

In all cases, such European laws shall be adopted after consultation of the Committee of the Regions and the Economic and Social Committee.

2.   The first provisions on the Structural Funds and the Cohesion Fund to be adopted following those in force on the date on which the Treaty establishing a Constitution for Europe is signed shall be established by a European law of the Council. The Council shall act unanimously after obtaining the consent of the European Parliament.

ARTICLE III-224

European laws shall establish implementing measures relating to the European Regional Development Fund. Such laws shall be adopted after consultation of the Committee of the Regions and the Economic and Social Committee.

With regard to the European Agricultural Guidance and Guarantee Fund, Guidance Section, and the European Social Fund, Articles III-231 and III-219(3) respectively shall apply.

SECTION 4

AGRICULTURE AND FISHERIES

ARTICLE III-225

The Union shall define and implement a common agriculture and fisheries policy.

"Agricultural products" means the products of the soil, of stockfarming and of fisheries and products of first-stage processing directly related to these products. References to the common agricultural policy or to agriculture, and the use of the term "agricultural", shall be understood as also referring to fisheries, having regard to the specific characteristics of this sector.

ARTICLE III-226

1.   The internal market shall extend to agriculture and trade in agricultural products.

2.   Save as otherwise provided in Articles III-227 to III-232, the rules laid down for the establishment and functioning of the internal market shall apply to agricultural products.

3.   The products listed in Annex I shall be subject to Articles III-227 to III-232.

4.   The operation and development of the internal market for agricultural products must be accompanied by a common agricultural policy.

ARTICLE III-227

1.   The objectives of the common agricultural policy shall be:

(a)   to increase agricultural productivity by promoting technical progress and by ensuring the rational development of agricultural production and the optimum utilisation of the factors of production, in particular labour;

(b)   thus to ensure a fair standard of living for the agricultural community, in particular by increasing the individual earnings of persons engaged in agriculture;

(c)   to stabilise markets;

(d)   to assure the availability of supplies;

(e)   to ensure that supplies reach consumers at reasonable prices.

2.   In working out the common agricultural policy and the special methods for its application, account shall be taken of:

(a)   the particular nature of agricultural activity, which results from the social structure of agriculture and from structural and natural disparities between the various agricultural regions;

(b)   the need to effect the appropriate adjustments by degrees;

(c) the fact that in the Member States agriculture constitutes a sector closely linked with the economy as a whole.

ARTICLE III-228

1. In order to attain the objectives set out in Article III-227, a common organisation of agricultural markets shall be established.

This organisation shall take one of the following forms, depending on the product concerned:

(a) common rules on competition;

(b) compulsory coordination of the various national market organisations;

(c) a European market organisation.

2. The common organisation established in accordance with paragraph 1 may include all measures required to attain the objectives set out in Article III-227, in particular regulation of prices, aids for the production and marketing of the various products, storage and carryover arrangements and common machinery for stabilising imports or exports.

The common organisation shall be limited to pursuit of the objectives set out in Article III-227 and shall exclude any discrimination between producers or consumers within the Union.

Any common price policy shall be based on common criteria and uniform methods of calculation.

3. In order to enable the common organisation referred to in paragraph 1 to attain its objectives, one or more agricultural guidance and guarantee funds may be set up.

ARTICLE III-229

To enable the objectives set out in Article III-227 to be attained, provision may be made within the framework of the common agricultural policy for measures such as:

(a) an effective coordination of efforts in the spheres of vocational training, of research and of the dissemination of agricultural knowledge; this may include joint financing of projects or institutions;

(b) joint measures to promote consumption of certain products.

ARTICLE III-230

1. The Section relating to rules on competition shall apply to production of and trade in agricultural products only to the extent determined by European laws or framework laws in accordance with Article III-231(2), having regard to the objectives set out in Article III-227.

2. The Council, on a proposal from the Commission, may adopt a European regulation or decision authorising the granting of aid:

(a) for the protection of enterprises handicapped by structural or natural conditions;

(b)   within the framework of economic development programmes.

ARTICLE III-231

1.   The Commission shall submit proposals for working out and implementing the common agricultural policy, including the replacement of the national organisations by one of the forms of common organisation provided for in Article III-228(1), and for implementing the measures referred to in this Section.

These proposals shall take account of the interdependence of the agricultural matters referred to in this Section.

2.   European laws or framework laws shall establish the common organisation of the market provided for in Article III-228(1) and the other provisions necessary for the pursuit of the objectives of the common agricultural policy and the common fisheries policy. They shall be adopted after consultation of the Economic and Social Committee.

3.   The Council, on a proposal from the Commission, shall adopt the European regulations or decisions on fixing prices, levies, aid and quantitative limitations and on the fixing and allocation of fishing opportunities.

4.   In accordance with paragraph 2, the national market organisations may be replaced by the common organisation provided for in Article III-228(1) if:

(a)   the common organisation offers Member States which are opposed to this measure and which have an organisation of their own for the production in question equivalent safeguards for the employment and standard of living of the producers concerned, account being taken of the adjustments that will be possible and the specialisation that will be needed with the passage of time, and

(b)   such an organisation ensures conditions for trade within the Union similar to those existing in a national market.

5.   If a common organisation for certain raw materials is established before a common organisation exists for the corresponding processed products, such raw materials as are used for processed products intended for export to third countries may be imported from outside the Union.

ARTICLE III-232

Where in a Member State a product is subject to a national market organisation or to internal rules having equivalent effect which affect the competitive position of similar production in another Member State, a countervailing charge shall be applied by Member States to imports of this product coming from the Member State where such organisation or rules exist, unless that State applies a countervailing charge on export.

The Commission shall adopt European regulations or decisions fixing the amount of these charges at the level required to redress the balance. It may also authorise other measures, the conditions and details of which it shall determine.

SECTION 5

ENVIRONMENT

ARTICLE III-233

1.   Union policy on the environment shall contribute to the pursuit of the following objectives:

(a)   preserving, protecting and improving the quality of the environment;

(b)   protecting human health;

(c)   prudent and rational utilisation of natural resources;

(d)   promoting measures at international level to deal with regional or worldwide environmental problems.

2.   Union policy on the environment shall aim at a high level of protection taking into account the diversity of situations in the various regions of the Union. It shall be based on the precautionary principle and on the principles that preventive action should be taken, that environmental damage should as a priority be rectified at source and that the polluter should pay.

In this context, harmonisation measures answering environmental protection requirements shall include, where appropriate, a safeguard clause allowing Member States to take provisional steps, for non-economic environmental reasons, subject to a procedure of inspection by the Union.

3.   In preparing its policy on the environment, the Union shall take account of:

(a)   available scientific and technical data;

(b)   environmental conditions in the various regions of the Union;

(c)   the potential benefits and costs of action or lack of action;

(d)   the economic and social development of the Union as a whole and the balanced development of its regions.

4.   Within their respective spheres of competence, the Union and the Member States shall cooperate with third countries and with the competent international organisations. The arrangements for the Union's cooperation may be the subject of agreements between the Union and the third parties concerned.

The first subparagraph shall be without prejudice to Member States' competence to negotiate in international bodies and to conclude international agreements.

ARTICLE III-234

1.   European laws or framework laws shall establish what action is to be taken in order to achieve the objectives referred to in Article III-233. They shall be adopted after consultation of the Committee of the Regions and the Economic and Social Committee.

2.   By way of derogation from paragraph 1 and without prejudice to Article III-172, the Council shall unanimously adopt European laws or framework laws establishing:

(a)   provisions primarily of a fiscal nature;

(b)   measures affecting:

    (i)   town and country planning;

    (ii)   quantitative management of water resources or affecting, directly or indirectly, the availability of those resources;

    (iii)   land use, with the exception of waste management;

(c)   measures significantly affecting a Member State's choice between different energy sources and the general structure of its energy supply.

The Council, on a proposal from the Commission, may unanimously adopt a European decision making the ordinary legislative procedure applicable to the matters referred to in the first subparagraph .

In all cases, the Council shall act after consulting the European Parliament, the Committee of the Regions and the Economic and Social Committee.

3.   European laws shall establish general action programmes which set out priority objectives to be attained. Such laws shall be adopted after consultation of the Committee of the Regions and the Economic and Social Committee.

The measures necessary for the implementation of these programmes shall be adopted under the terms of paragraph 1 or 2, as the case may be.

4.   Without prejudice to certain measures adopted by the Union, the Member States shall finance and implement the environment policy.

5.   Without prejudice to the principle that the polluter should pay, if a measure based on paragraph 1 involves costs deemed disproportionate for the public authorities of a Member State, such measure shall provide in appropriate form for:

(a)   temporary derogations, and/or

(b)   financial support from the Cohesion Fund.

6.   The protective measures adopted pursuant to this Article shall not prevent any Member State from maintaining or introducing more stringent protective measures. Such measures must be compatible with the Constitution. They shall be notified to the Commission.

SECTION 6

CONSUMER PROTECTION

ARTICLE III-235

1.   In order to promote the interests of consumers and to ensure a high level of consumer protection, the Union shall contribute to protecting the health, safety and economic interests of consumers, as well as to promoting their right to information, education and to organise themselves in order to safeguard their interests.

2.   The Union shall contribute to the attainment of the objectives referred to in paragraph 1 through:

(a)   measures adopted pursuant to Article III-172 in the context of the establishment and functioning of the internal market;

(b)   measures which support, supplement and monitor the policy pursued by the Member States.

3.   European laws or framework laws shall establish the measures referred to in paragraph 2(b). Such laws shall be adopted after consultation of the Economic and Social Committee.

4.   Acts adopted pursuant to paragraph 3 shall not prevent any Member State from maintaining or introducing more stringent protective provisions. Such provisions must be compatible with the Constitution. They shall be notified to the Commission.

SECTION 7

TRANSPORT

ARTICLE III-236

1.   The objectives of the Constitution shall, in matters governed by this Section, be pursued within the framework of a common transport policy.

2.   European laws or framework laws shall implement paragraph 1, taking into account the distinctive features of transport. They shall be adopted after consultation of the Committee of the Regions and the Economic and Social Committee.

Such European laws or framework laws shall establish:

(a)   common rules applicable to international transport to or from the territory of a Member State or passing across the territory of one or more Member States;

(b)   the conditions under which non-resident carriers may operate transport services within a Member State;

(c)   measures to improve transport safety;

(d)   any other appropriate measure.

3.   When the European laws or framework laws referred to in paragraph 2 are adopted, account shall be taken of cases where their application might seriously affect the standard of living and level of employment in certain regions, and the operation of transport facilities.

ARTICLE III-237

Until the European laws or framework laws referred to in Article III-236(2) have been adopted, no Member State may, unless the Council has unanimously adopted a European decision granting a derogation, make the various provisions governing the subject on 1 January 1958 or, for acceding States, the date of their accession less favourable in their direct or indirect effect on carriers of other Member States as compared with carriers who are nationals of that State.

ARTICLE III-238

Aids shall be compatible with the Constitution if they meet the needs of coordination of transport or if they represent reimbursement for the discharge of certain obligations inherent in the concept of a public service.

ARTICLE III-239

Any measures adopted within the framework of the Constitution in respect of transport rates and conditions shall take account of the economic circumstances of carriers.

ARTICLE III-240

1.   In the case of transport within the Union, discrimination which takes the form of carriers charging different rates and imposing different conditions for the carriage of the same goods over the same transport links on grounds of the Member State of origin or of destination of the goods in question shall be prohibited.

2.   Paragraph 1 shall not prevent the adoption of other European laws or framework laws pursuant to Article III-236(2).

3.   The Council, on a proposal from the Commission, shall adopt European regulations or decisions for implementing paragraph 1. It shall act after consulting the European Parliament and the Economic and Social Committee.

The Council may in particular adopt the European regulations and decisions needed to enable the institutions to secure compliance with the rule laid down in paragraph 1 and to ensure that users benefit from it to the full.

4.   The Commission, acting on its own initiative or on application by a Member State, shall investigate any cases of discrimination falling within paragraph 1 and, after consulting any Member State concerned, adopt the necessary European decisions within the framework of the European regulations and decisions referred to in paragraph 3.

ARTICLE III-241

1.   The imposition by a Member State, in respect of transport operations carried out within the Union, of rates and conditions involving any element of support or protection in the interest of one or more particular undertakings or industries shall be prohibited, unless authorised by a European decision of the Commission.

2.   The Commission, acting on its own initiative or on application by a Member State, shall examine the rates and conditions referred to in paragraph 1, taking account in particular of the requirements of an appropriate regional economic policy, the needs of underdeveloped areas and the problems of areas seriously affected by political circumstances on the one hand, and of the effects of such rates and conditions on competition between the different modes of transport on the other.

After consulting each Member State concerned, the Commission shall adopt the necessary European decisions.

3.   The prohibition provided for in paragraph 1 shall not apply to tariffs fixed to meet competition.

ARTICLE III-242

Charges or dues in respect of the crossing of frontiers which are charged by a carrier in addition to the transport rates shall not exceed a reasonable level after taking the costs actually incurred thereby into account.

Member States shall endeavour to reduce these costs.

The Commission may make recommendations to Member States for the application of this Article.

ARTICLE III-243

The provisions of this Section shall not form an obstacle to the application of measures taken in the Federal Republic of Germany to the extent that such measures are required in order to compensate for the economic disadvantages caused by the division of Germany to the economy of certain areas of the Federal Republic affected by that division. Five years after the entry into force of the Treaty establishing a Constitution for Europe, the Council, acting on a proposal from the Commission, may adopt a European decision repealing this Article.

ARTICLE III-244

An Advisory Committee consisting of experts designated by the governments of the Member States shall be attached to the Commission. The Commission, whenever it considers it desirable, shall consult the Committee on transport matters.

ARTICLE III-245

1.   This Section shall apply to transport by rail, road and inland waterway.

2.   European laws or framework laws may lay down appropriate measures for sea and air transport. They shall be adopted after consultation of the Committee of the Regions and the Economic and Social Committee.

SECTION 8

TRANS-EUROPEAN NETWORKS

ARTICLE III-246

1.   To help achieve the objectives referred to in Articles III-130 and III-220 and to enable citizens of the Union, economic operators and regional and local communities to derive full benefit from the setting-up of an area without internal frontiers, the Union shall contribute to the establishment and development of trans-European networks in the areas of transport, telecommunications and energy infrastructures.

2.   Within the framework of a system of open and competitive markets, action by the Union shall aim at promoting the interconnection and interoperability of national networks as well as access to such networks. It shall take account in particular of the need to link island, landlocked and peripheral regions with the central regions of the Union.

ARTICLE III-247

1.   In order to achieve the objectives referred to in Article III-246, the Union:

(a)   shall establish a series of guidelines covering the objectives, priorities and broad lines of measures envisaged in the sphere of trans-European networks; these guidelines shall identify projects of common interest;

(b)   shall implement any measures that may prove necessary to ensure the interoperability of the networks, in particular in the field of technical standardisation;

(c)   may support projects of common interest supported by Member States, which are identified in the framework of the guidelines referred to in point (a), particularly through feasibility studies, loan guarantees or interest-rate subsidies; the Union may also contribute, through the Cohesion Fund, to the financing of specific projects in Member States in the area of transport infrastructure.

The Union's activities shall take into account the potential economic viability of the projects.

2.   European laws or framework laws shall establish the guidelines and other measures referred to in paragraph 1. Such laws shall be adopted after consultation of the Committee of the Regions and the Economic and Social Committee.

Guidelines and projects of common interest which relate to the territory of a Member State shall require the agreement of that Member State.

3.   Member States shall, in liaison with the Commission, coordinate among themselves the policies pursued at national level which may have a significant impact on the achievement of the objectives referred to in Article III-246. The Commission may, in close cooperation with the Member States, take any useful initiative to promote such coordination.

4.   The Union may cooperate with third countries to promote projects of mutual interest and to ensure the interoperability of networks.

SECTION 9

RESEARCH AND TECHNOLOGICAL DEVELOPMENT AND SPACE

ARTICLE III-248

1.   The Union shall aim to strengthen its scientific and technological bases by achieving a European research area in which researchers, scientific knowledge and technology circulate freely, and encourage it to become more competitive, including in its industry, while promoting all the research activities deemed necessary by virtue of other Chapters of the Constitution.

2.   For the purposes referred to in paragraph 1 the Union shall, throughout the Union, encourage undertakings, including small and medium-sized undertakings, research centres and universities in their research and technological development activities of high quality. It shall support their efforts to cooperate with one another, aiming, notably, at permitting researchers to cooperate freely across borders and at enabling undertakings to exploit the internal market potential, in particular through the opening-up of national public contracts, the definition of common standards and the removal of legal and fiscal obstacles to that cooperation.

3.   All the Union's activities in the area of research and technological development, including demonstration projects, shall be decided on and implemented in accordance with this Section.

ARTICLE III-249

In pursuing the objectives referred to in Article III-248, the Union shall carry out the following activities, complementing the activities carried out in the Member States:

(a)   implementation of research, technological development and demonstration programmes, by promoting cooperation with and between undertakings, research centres and universities;

(b)   promotion of cooperation in the field of the Union's research, technological development and demonstration with third countries and international organisations;

(c)   dissemination and optimisation of the results of activities in the Union's research, technological development and demonstration;

(d)   stimulation of the training and mobility of researchers in the Union.

ARTICLE III-250

1.   The Union and the Member States shall coordinate their research and technological development activities so as to ensure that national policies and the Union's policy are mutually consistent.

2.   In close cooperation with the Member States, the Commission may take any useful initiative to promote the coordination referred to in paragraph 1, in particular initiatives aiming at the establishment of guidelines and indicators, the organisation of exchange of best practice, and the preparation of the necessary elements for periodic monitoring and evaluation. The European Parliament shall be kept fully informed.

ARTICLE III-251

1.   European laws shall establish a multiannual framework programme, setting out all the activities financed by the Union. Such laws shall be adopted after consultation of the Economic and Social Committee.

The framework programme shall:

(a)   establish the scientific and technological objectives to be achieved by the activities provided for in Article III-249 and lay down the relevant priorities;

(b)   indicate the broad lines of such activities;

(c)   lay down the maximum overall amount and the detailed rules for the Union's financial participation in the framework programme and the respective shares in each of the activities provided for.

2.   The multiannual framework programme shall be adapted or supplemented as the situation changes.

3.   A European law of the Council shall establish specific programmes to implement the multiannual framework programme within each activity. Each specific programme shall define the detailed rules for implementing it, fix its duration and provide for the means deemed necessary. The sum of the amounts deemed necessary, fixed in the specific programmes, shall not exceed the overall maximum amount fixed for the framework programme and each activity. Such a law shall be adopted after consulting the European Parliament and the Economic and Social Committee.

4.   As a complement to the activities planned in the multiannual framework programme, European laws shall establish the measures necessary for the implementation of the European research area. Such laws shall be adopted after consulting the Economic and Social Committee.

ARTICLE III-252

1.   For the implementation of the multiannual framework programme, European laws or framework laws shall establish:

(a)   the rules for the participation of undertakings, research centres and universities;

(b)   the rules governing the dissemination of research results.

Such European laws or framework laws shall be adopted after consultation of the Economic and Social Committee.

2.   In implementing the multiannual framework programme, European laws may establish supplementary programmes involving the participation of certain Member States only, which shall finance them subject to possible participation by the Union.

Such European laws shall determine the rules applicable to supplementary programmes, particularly as regards the dissemination of knowledge as well as access by other Member States. They shall be adopted after consultation of the Economic and Social Committee and with the agreement of the Member States concerned.

3.   In implementing the multiannual framework programme, European laws may make provision, in agreement with the Member States concerned, for participation in research and development programmes undertaken by several Member States, including participation in the structures created for the execution of those programmes.

Such European laws shall be adopted after consultation of the Economic and Social Committee.

4.   In implementing the multiannual framework programme the Union may make provision for cooperation in the Union's research, technological development and demonstration with third countries or international organisations.

The detailed arrangements for such cooperation may be the subject of agreements between the Union and the third parties concerned.

ARTICLE III-253

The Council, on a proposal from the Commission, may adopt European regulations or decisions to set up joint undertakings or any other structure necessary for the efficient execution of the Union's research, technological development and demonstration programmes. It shall act after consulting the European Parliament and the Economic and Social Committee.

ARTICLE III-254

1.   To promote scientific and technical progress, industrial competitiveness and the implementation of its policies, the Union shall draw up a European space policy. To this end, it may promote joint initiatives, support research and technological development and coordinate the efforts needed for the exploration and exploitation of space.

2.   To contribute to attaining the objectives referred to in paragraph 1, European laws or framework laws shall establish the necessary measures, which may take the form of a European space programme.

3.   The Union shall establish any appropriate relations with the European Space Agency.

ARTICLE III-255

At the beginning of each year the Commission shall send a report to the European Parliament and the Council. The report shall include information on activities relating to research, technological development and the dissemination of results during the previous year, and the work programme for the current year.

SECTION 10

ENERGY

ARTICLE III-256

1.   In the context of the establishment and functioning of the internal market and with regard for the need to preserve and improve the environment, Union policy on energy shall aim to:

(a)   ensure the functioning of the energy market;

(b)   ensure security of energy supply in the Union, and

(c)   promote energy efficiency and energy saving and the development of new and renewable forms of energy.

2.   Without prejudice to the application of other provisions of the Constitution, the objectives in paragraph 1 shall be achieved by measures enacted in European laws or framework laws. Such laws or framework laws shall be adopted after consultation of the Committee of the Regions and the Economic and Social Committee.

Such European laws or framework laws shall not affect a Member State's right to determine the conditions for exploiting its energy resources, its choice between different energy sources and the general structure of its energy supply, without prejudice to Article III-234(2)(c).

3.   By way of derogation from paragraph 2, a European law or framework law of the Council shall establish the measures referred to therein when they are primarily of a fiscal nature. The Council shall act unanimously after consulting the European Parliament.

CHAPTER IV

AREA OF FREEDOM, SECURITY AND JUSTICE

SECTION 1

GENERAL PROVISIONS

ARTICLE III-257

1. The Union shall constitute an area of freedom, security and justice with respect for fundamental rights and the different legal systems and traditions of the Member States.

2. It shall ensure the absence of internal border controls for persons and shall frame a common policy on asylum, immigration and external border control, based on solidarity between Member States, which is fair towards third-country nationals. For the purpose of this Chapter, stateless persons shall be treated as third-country nationals.

3. The Union shall endeavour to ensure a high level of security through measures to prevent and combat crime, racism and xenophobia, and through measures for coordination and cooperation between police and judicial authorities and other competent authorities, as well as through the mutual recognition of judgments in criminal matters and, if necessary, through the approximation of criminal laws.

4. The Union shall facilitate access to justice, in particular through the principle of mutual recognition of judicial and extrajudicial decisions in civil matters.

ARTICLE III-258

The European Council shall define the strategic guidelines for legislative and operational planning within the area of freedom, security and justice.

ARTICLE III-259

National Parliaments shall ensure that the proposals and legislative initiatives submitted under Sections 4 and 5 of this Chapter comply with the principle of subsidiarity, in accordance with the arrangements laid down by the Protocol on the application of the principles of subsidiarity and proportionality.

ARTICLE III-260

Without prejudice to Articles III-360 to III-362, the Council may, on a proposal from the Commission, adopt European regulations or decisions laying down the arrangements whereby Member States, in collaboration with the Commission, conduct objective and impartial evaluation of the implementation of the Union policies referred to in this Chapter by Member States' authorities, in particular in order to facilitate full application of the principle of mutual recognition. The European Parliament and national Parliaments shall be informed of the content and results of the evaluation.

ARTICLE III-261

A standing committee shall be set up within the Council in order to ensure that operational cooperation on internal security is promoted and strengthened within the Union. Without prejudice to Article III-344, it shall facilitate coordination of the action of Member States' competent authorities. Representatives of the Union bodies, offices and agencies concerned may be involved in the proceedings of this committee. The European Parliament and national Parliaments shall be kept informed of the proceedings.

ARTICLE III-262

This Chapter shall not affect the exercise of the responsibilities incumbent upon Member States with regard to the maintenance of law and order and the safeguarding of internal security.

ARTICLE III-263

The Council shall adopt European regulations to ensure administrative cooperation between the relevant departments of the Member States in the areas covered by this Chapter, as well as between those departments and the Commission. It shall act on a Commission proposal, subject to Article III-264, and after consulting the European Parliament.

ARTICLE III-264

The acts referred to in Sections 4 and 5, together with the European regulations referred to in Article III-263 which ensure administrative cooperation in the areas covered by these Sections, shall be adopted:

(a)   on a proposal from the Commission, or

(b)   on the initiative of a quarter of the Member States.

SECTION 2

POLICIES ON BORDER CHECKS, ASYLUM AND IMMIGRATION

ARTICLE III-265

1.   The Union shall develop a policy with a view to:

(a)   ensuring the absence of any controls on persons, whatever their nationality, when crossing internal borders;

(b)   carrying out checks on persons and efficient monitoring of the crossing of external borders;

(c)   the gradual introduction of an integrated management system for external borders.

2.   For the purposes of paragraph 1, European laws or framework laws shall establish measures concerning:

(a)   the common policy on visas and other short-stay residence permits;

(b)   the checks to which persons crossing external borders are subject;

(c)   the conditions under which nationals of third countries shall have the freedom to travel within the Union for a short period;

(d)   any measure necessary for the gradual establishment of an integrated management system for external borders;

(e)   the absence of any controls on persons, whatever their nationality, when crossing internal borders.

3.   This Article shall not affect the competence of the Member States concerning the geographical demarcation of their borders, in accordance with international law.

ARTICLE III-266

1.   The Union shall develop a common policy on asylum, subsidiary protection and temporary protection with a view to offering appropriate status to any third-country national requiring international protection and ensuring compliance with the principle of non-refoulement. This policy must be in accordance with the Geneva Convention of 28 July 1951 and the Protocol of 31 January 1967 relating to the status of refugees, and other relevant treaties.

2.   For the purposes of paragraph 1, European laws or framework laws shall lay down measures for a common European asylum system comprising:

(a)   a uniform status of asylum for nationals of third countries, valid throughout the Union;

(b)   a uniform status of subsidiary protection for nationals of third countries who, without obtaining European asylum, are in need of international protection;

(c)   a common system of temporary protection for displaced persons in the event of a massive inflow;

(d)   common procedures for the granting and withdrawing of uniform asylum or subsidiary protection status;

(e)   criteria and mechanisms for determining which Member State is responsible for considering an application for asylum or subsidiary protection;

(f)   standards concerning the conditions for the reception of applicants for asylum or subsidiary protection;

(g)   partnership and cooperation with third countries for the purpose of managing inflows of people applying for asylum or subsidiary or temporary protection.

3.   In the event of one or more Member States being confronted by an emergency situation characterised by a sudden inflow of nationals of third countries, the Council, on a proposal from the Commission, may adopt European regulations or decisions comprising provisional measures for the benefit of the Member State(s) concerned. It shall act after consulting the European Parliament.

ARTICLE III-267

1.   The Union shall develop a common immigration policy aimed at ensuring, at all stages, the efficient management of migration flows, fair treatment of third-country nationals residing legally in Member States, and the prevention of, and enhanced measures to combat, illegal immigration and trafficking in human beings.

2.   For the purposes of paragraph 1, European laws or framework laws shall establish measures in the following areas:

(a)   the conditions of entry and residence, and standards on the issue by Member States of long-term visas and residence permits, including those for the purpose of family reunion;

(b)   the definition of the rights of third-country nationals residing legally in a Member State, including the conditions governing freedom of movement and of residence in other Member States;

(c)   illegal immigration and unauthorised residence, including removal and repatriation of persons residing without authorisation;

(d)   combating trafficking in persons, in particular women and children.

3.   The Union may conclude agreements with third countries for the readmission to their countries of origin or provenance of third-country nationals who do not or who no longer fulfil the conditions for entry, presence or residence in the territory of one of the Member States.

4.   European laws or framework laws may establish measures to provide incentives and support for the action of Member States with a view to promoting the integration of third-country nationals residing legally in their territories, excluding any harmonisation of the laws and regulations of the Member States.

5.   This Article shall not affect the right of Member States to determine volumes of admission of third-country nationals coming from third countries to their territory in order to seek work, whether employed or self-employed.

ARTICLE III-268

The policies of the Union set out in this Section and their implementation shall be governed by the principle of solidarity and fair sharing of responsibility, including its financial implications, between the Member States. Whenever necessary, the Union acts adopted pursuant to this Section shall contain appropriate measures to give effect to this principle.

SECTION 3

JUDICIAL COOPERATION IN CIVIL MATTERS

ARTICLE III-269

1.   The Union shall develop judicial cooperation in civil matters having cross-border implications, based on the principle of mutual recognition of judgments and decisions in extrajudicial cases. Such cooperation may include the adoption of measures for the approximation of the laws and regulations of the Member States.

2.   For the purposes of paragraph 1, European laws or framework laws shall establish measures, particularly when necessary for the proper functioning of the internal market, aimed at ensuring:

(a)   the mutual recognition and enforcement between Member States of judgments and decisions in extrajudicial cases;

(b)   the cross-border service of judicial and extrajudicial documents;

(c)   the compatibility of the rules applicable in the Member States concerning conflict of laws and of jurisdiction;

(d)   cooperation in the taking of evidence;

(e)   effective access to justice;

(f)   the elimination of obstacles to the proper functioning of civil proceedings, if necessary by promoting the compatibility of the rules on civil procedure applicable in the Member States;

(g)   the development of alternative methods of dispute settlement;

(h)   support for the training of the judiciary and judicial staff.

3.   Notwithstanding paragraph 2, a European law or framework law of the Council shall establish measures concerning family law with cross-border implications. The Council shall act unanimously after consulting the European Parliament.

The Council, on a proposal from the Commission, may adopt a European decision determining those aspects of family law with cross-border implications which may be the subject of acts adopted by the ordinary legislative procedure. The Council shall act unanimously after consulting the European Parliament.

SECTION 4

JUDICIAL COOPERATION IN CRIMINAL MATTERS

ARTICLE III-270

1.   Judicial cooperation in criminal matters in the Union shall be based on the principle of mutual recognition of judgments and judicial decisions and shall include the approximation of the laws and regulations of the Member States in the areas referred to in paragraph 2 and in Article III-271.

European laws or framework laws shall establish measures to:

(a)   lay down rules and procedures for ensuring recognition throughout the Union of all forms of judgments and judicial decisions;

(b)   prevent and settle conflicts of jurisdiction between Member States;

(c)   support the training of the judiciary and judicial staff;

(d)   facilitate cooperation between judicial or equivalent authorities of the Member States in relation to proceedings in criminal matters and the enforcement of decisions.

2.   To the extent necessary to facilitate mutual recognition of judgments and judicial decisions and police and judicial cooperation in criminal matters having a cross-border dimension, European framework laws may establish minimum rules. Such rules shall take into account the differences between the legal traditions and systems of the Member States.

They shall concern:

(a)   mutual admissibility of evidence between Member States;

(b)   the rights of individuals in criminal procedure;

(c)   the rights of victims of crime;

(d)   any other specific aspects of criminal procedure which the Council has identified in advance by a European decision; for the adoption of such a decision, the Council shall act unanimously after obtaining the consent of the European Parliament.

Adoption of the minimum rules referred to in this paragraph shall not prevent Member States from maintaining or introducing a higher level of protection for individuals.

3.   Where a member of the Council considers that a draft European framework law as referred to in paragraph 2 would affect fundamental aspects of its criminal justice system, it may request that the draft framework law be referred to the European Council. In that case, the procedure referred to in Article III-396 shall be suspended. After discussion, the European Council shall, within four months of this suspension, either:

(a)   refer the draft back to the Council, which shall terminate the suspension of the procedure referred to in Article III-396, or

(b)   request the Commission or the group of Member States from which the draft originates to submit a new draft; in that case, the act originally proposed shall be deemed not to have been adopted.

4.   If, by the end of the period referred to in paragraph 3, either no action has been taken by the European Council or if, within 12 months from the submission of a new draft under paragraph 3(b), the European framework law has not been adopted, and at least one third of the Member States wish to establish enhanced cooperation on the basis of the draft framework law concerned, they shall notify the European Parliament, the Council and the Commission accordingly.

In such a case, the authorisation to proceed with enhanced cooperation referred to in Articles I-44(2) and III-419(1) shall be deemed to be granted and the provisions on enhanced cooperation shall apply.

ARTICLE III-271

1.   European framework laws may establish minimum rules concerning the definition of criminal offences and sanctions in the areas of particularly serious crime with a cross-border dimension resulting from the nature or impact of such offences or from a special need to combat them on a common basis.

These areas of crime are the following: terrorism, trafficking in human beings and sexual exploitation of women and children, illicit drug trafficking, illicit arms trafficking, money laundering, corruption, counterfeiting of means of payment, computer crime and organised crime.

On the basis of developments in crime, the Council may adopt a European decision identifying other areas of crime that meet the criteria specified in this paragraph. It shall act unanimously after obtaining the consent of the European Parliament.

2.   If the approximation of criminal laws and regulations of the Member States proves essential to ensure the effective implementation of a Union policy in an area which has been subject to harmonisation measures, European framework laws may establish minimum rules with regard to the definition of criminal offences and sanctions in the area concerned. Such framework laws shall be adopted by the same procedure as was followed for the adoption of the harmonisation measures in question, without prejudice to Article III-264.

3.   Where a member of the Council considers that a draft European framework law as referred to in paragraph 1 or 2 would affect fundamental aspects of its criminal justice system, it may request that the draft framework law be referred to the European Council. In that case, where the procedure referred to in Article III-396 is applicable, it shall be suspended. After discussion, the European Council shall, within four months of this suspension, either:

(a)   refer the draft back to the Council, which shall terminate the suspension of the procedure referred to in Article III-396 where it is applicable, or

(b)   request the Commission or the group of Member States from which the draft originates to submit a new draft; in that case, the act originally proposed shall be deemed not to have been adopted.

4.   If, by the end of the period referred to in paragraph 3, either no action has been taken by the European Council or if, within 12 months from the submission of a new draft under paragraph 3(b), the European framework law has not been adopted, and at least one third of

the Member States wish to establish enhanced cooperation on the basis of the draft framework law concerned, they shall notify the European Parliament, the Council and the Commission accordingly.

In such a case, the authorisation to proceed with enhanced cooperation referred to in Articles I-44(2) and III-419(1) shall be deemed to be granted and the provisions on enhanced cooperation shall apply.

ARTICLE III-272

European laws or framework laws may establish measures to promote and support the action of Member States in the field of crime prevention, excluding any harmonisation of the laws and regulations of the Member States.

ARTICLE III-273

1.   Eurojust's mission shall be to support and strengthen coordination and cooperation between national investigating and prosecuting authorities in relation to serious crime affecting two or more Member States or requiring a prosecution on common bases, on the basis of operations conducted and information supplied by the Member States' authorities and by Europol.

In this context, European laws shall determine Eurojust's structure, operation, field of action and tasks. Those tasks may include:

(a)   the initiation of criminal investigations, as well as proposing the initiation of prosecutions, conducted by competent national authorities, particularly those relating to offences against the financial interests of the Union;

(b)   the coordination of investigations and prosecutions referred to in point (a);

(c)   the strengthening of judicial cooperation, including by resolution of conflicts of jurisdiction and by close cooperation with the European Judicial Network.

European laws shall also determine arrangements for involving the European Parliament and national Parliaments in the evaluation of Eurojust's activities.

2.   In the prosecutions referred to in paragraph 1, and without prejudice to Article III-274, formal acts of judicial procedure shall be carried out by the competent national officials.

ARTICLE III-274

1.   In order to combat crimes affecting the financial interests of the Union, a European law of the Council may establish a European Public Prosecutor's Office from Eurojust. The Council shall act unanimously after obtaining the consent of the European Parliament.

2.   The European Public Prosecutor's Office shall be responsible for investigating, prosecuting and bringing to judgment, where appropriate in liaison with Europol, the perpetrators of, and accomplices in, offences against the Union's financial interests, as determined by the European

law provided for in paragraph 1. It shall exercise the functions of prosecutor in the competent courts of the Member States in relation to such offences.

3.   The European law referred to in paragraph 1 shall determine the general rules applicable to the European Public Prosecutor's Office, the conditions governing the performance of its functions, the rules of procedure applicable to its activities, as well as those governing the admissibility of evidence, and the rules applicable to the judicial review of procedural measures taken by it in the performance of its functions.

4.   The European Council may, at the same time or subsequently, adopt a European decision amending paragraph 1 in order to extend the powers of the European Public Prosecutor's Office to include serious crime having a cross-border dimension and amending accordingly paragraph 2 as regards the perpetrators of, and accomplices in, serious crimes affecting more than one Member State. The European Council shall act unanimously after obtaining the consent of the European Parliament and after consulting the Commission.

SECTION 5

POLICE COOPERATION

ARTICLE III-275

1.   The Union shall establish police cooperation involving all the Member States' competent authorities, including police, customs and other specialised law enforcement services in relation to the prevention, detection and investigation of criminal offences.

2.   For the purposes of paragraph 1, European laws or framework laws may establish measures concerning:

(a)   the collection, storage, processing, analysis and exchange of relevant information;

(b)   support for the training of staff, and cooperation on the exchange of staff, on equipment and on research into crime-detection;

(c)   common investigative techniques in relation to the detection of serious forms of organised crime.

3.   A European law or framework law of the Council may establish measures concerning operational cooperation between the authorities referred to in this Article. The Council shall act unanimously after consulting the European Parliament.

ARTICLE III-276

1.   Europol's mission shall be to support and strengthen action by the Member States' police authorities and other law enforcement services and their mutual cooperation in preventing and combating serious crime affecting two or more Member States, terrorism and forms of crime which affect a common interest covered by a Union policy.

2.   European laws shall determine Europol's structure, operation, field of action and tasks. These tasks may include:

(a)   the collection, storage, processing, analysis and exchange of information forwarded particularly by the authorities of the Member States or third countries or bodies;

(b)   the coordination, organisation and implementation of investigative and operational action carried out jointly with the Member States' competent authorities or in the context of joint investigative teams, where appropriate in liaison with Eurojust.

European laws shall also lay down the procedures for scrutiny of Europol's activities by the European Parliament, together with national Parliaments.

3.   Any operational action by Europol must be carried out in liaison and in agreement with the authorities of the Member State or States whose territory is concerned. The application of coercive measures shall be the exclusive responsibility of the competent national authorities.

ARTICLE III-277

A European law or framework law of the Council shall lay down the conditions and limitations under which the competent authorities of the Member States referred to in Articles III-270 and III-275 may operate in the territory of another Member State in liaison and in agreement with the authorities of that State. The Council shall act unanimously after consulting the European Parliament.

CHAPTER V

AREAS WHERE THE UNION MAY TAKE COORDINATING, COMPLEMENTARY OR SUPPORTING ACTION

SECTION 1

PUBLIC HEALTH

ARTICLE III-278

1.   A high level of human health protection shall be ensured in the definition and implementation of all the Union's policies and activities.

Action by the Union, which shall complement national policies, shall be directed towards improving public health, preventing human illness and diseases, and obviating sources of danger to physical and mental health. Such action shall cover:

(a)   the fight against the major health scourges, by promoting research into their causes, their transmission and their prevention, as well as health information and education;

(b)   monitoring, early warning of and combating serious cross-border threats to health.

The Union shall complement the Member States' action in reducing drug-related health damage, including information and prevention.

2.   The Union shall encourage cooperation between the Member States in the areas referred to in this Article and, if necessary, lend support to their action. It shall in particular encourage cooperation between the Member States to improve the complementarity of their health services in cross-border areas.

Member States shall, in liaison with the Commission, coordinate among themselves their policies and programmes in the areas referred to in paragraph 1. The Commission may, in close contact with the Member States, take any useful initiative to promote such coordination, in particular initiatives aiming at the establishment of guidelines and indicators, the organisation of exchange of best practice, and the preparation of the necessary elements for periodic monitoring and evaluation. The European Parliament shall be kept fully informed.

3.   The Union and the Member States shall foster cooperation with third countries and the competent international organisations in the sphere of public health.

4.   By way of derogation from Article I-12(5) and Article I-17(a) and in accordance with Article I-14(2)(k), European laws or framework laws shall contribute to the achievement of the objectives referred to in this Article by establishing the following measures in order to meet common safety concerns:

(a)   measures setting high standards of quality and safety of organs and substances of human origin, blood and blood derivatives; these measures shall not prevent any Member State from maintaining or introducing more stringent protective measures;

(b)   measures in the veterinary and phytosanitary fields which have as their direct objective the protection of public health;

(c)   measures setting high standards of quality and safety for medicinal products and devices for medical use;

(d)   measures concerning monitoring, early warning of and combating serious cross-border threats to health.

Such European laws or framework laws shall be adopted after consultation of the Committee of the Regions and the Economic and Social Committee.

5.   European laws or framework laws may also establish incentive measures designed to protect and improve human health and in particular to combat the major cross-border health scourges, as well as measures which have as their direct objective the protection of public health regarding tobacco and the abuse of alcohol, excluding any harmonisation of the laws and regulations of the Member States. They shall be adopted after consultation of the Committee of the Regions and the Economic and Social Committee.

6.   For the purposes of this Article, the Council, on a proposal from the Commission, may also adopt recommendations.

7.   Union action shall respect the responsibilities of the Member States for the definition of their health policy and for the organisation and delivery of health services and medical care. The responsibilities of the Member States shall include the management of health services and medical care and the allocation of the resources assigned to them. The measures referred to in

paragraph 4(a) shall not affect national provisions on the donation or medical use of organs and blood.

SECTION 2

INDUSTRY

ARTICLE III-279

1.   The Union and the Member States shall ensure that the conditions necessary for the competitiveness of the Union's industry exist.

For that purpose, in accordance with a system of open and competitive markets, their action shall be aimed at:

(a)   speeding up the adjustment of industry to structural changes;

(b)   encouraging an environment favourable to initiative and to the development of undertakings throughout the Union, particularly small and medium-sized undertakings;

(c)   encouraging an environment favourable to cooperation between undertakings;

(d)   fostering better exploitation of the industrial potential of policies of innovation, research and technological development.

2.   The Member States shall consult each other in liaison with the Commission and, where necessary, shall coordinate their action. The Commission may take any useful initiative to promote such coordination, in particular initiatives aiming at the establishment of guidelines and indicators, the organisation of exchange of best practice, and the preparation of the necessary elements for periodic monitoring and evaluation. The European Parliament shall be kept fully informed.

3.   The Union shall contribute to the achievement of the objectives set out in paragraph 1 through the policies and activities it pursues under other provisions of the Constitution. European laws or framework laws may establish specific measures in support of action taken in the Member States to achieve the objectives set out in paragraph 1, excluding any harmonisation of the laws and regulations of the Member States. They shall be adopted after consultation of the Economic and Social Committee.

This Section shall not provide a basis for the introduction by the Union of any measure which could lead to distortion of competition or contains tax provisions or provisions relating to the rights and interests of employed persons.

SECTION 3

CULTURE

ARTICLE III-280

1.   The Union shall contribute to the flowering of the cultures of the Member States, while respecting their national and regional diversity and at the same time bringing the common cultural heritage to the fore.

2.   Action by the Union shall be aimed at encouraging cooperation between Member States and, if necessary, supporting and complementing their action in the following areas:

(a)   improvement of the knowledge and dissemination of the culture and history of the European peoples;

(b)   conservation and safeguarding of cultural heritage of European significance;

(c)   non-commercial cultural exchanges;

(d)   artistic and literary creation, including in the audiovisual sector.

3.   The Union and the Member States shall foster cooperation with third countries and the competent international organisations in the sphere of culture, in particular the Council of Europe.

4.   The Union shall take cultural aspects into account in its action under other provisions of the Constitution, in particular in order to respect and to promote the diversity of its cultures.

5.   In order to contribute to the achievement of the objectives referred to in this Article:

(a)   European laws or framework laws shall establish incentive measures, excluding any harmonisation of the laws and regulations of the Member States. They shall be adopted after consultation of the Committee of the Regions;

(b)   the Council, on a proposal from the Commission, shall adopt recommendations.

SECTION 4

TOURISM

ARTICLE III-281

1.   The Union shall complement the action of the Member States in the tourism sector, in particular by promoting the competitiveness of Union undertakings in that sector.

To that end, Union action shall be aimed at:

(a)   encouraging the creation of a favourable environment for the development of undertakings in this sector;

(b)   promoting cooperation between the Member States, particularly by the exchange of good practice;

2.   European laws or framework laws shall establish specific measures to complement actions within the Member States to achieve the objectives referred to in this Article, excluding any harmonisation of the laws and regulations of the Member States.

SECTION 5

EDUCATION, YOUTH, SPORT AND VOCATIONAL TRAINING

ARTICLE III-282

1.   The Union shall contribute to the development of quality education by encouraging cooperation between Member States and, if necessary, by supporting and complementing their action. It shall fully respect the responsibility of the Member States for the content of teaching and the organisation of education systems and their cultural and linguistic diversity.

The Union shall contribute to the promotion of European sporting issues, while taking account of the specific nature of sport, its structures based on voluntary activity and its social and educational function.

Union action shall be aimed at:

(a)   developing the European dimension in education, particularly through the teaching and dissemination of the languages of the Member States;

(b)   encouraging mobility of students and teachers, inter alia by encouraging the academic recognition of diplomas and periods of study;

(c)   promoting cooperation between educational establishments;

(d)   developing exchanges of information and experience on issues common to the education systems of the Member States;

(e)   encouraging the development of youth exchanges and of exchanges of socio-educational instructors and encouraging the participation of young people in democratic life in Europe;

(f)   encouraging the development of distance education;

(g)   developing the European dimension in sport, by promoting fairness and openness in sporting competitions and cooperation between bodies responsible for sports, and by protecting the physical and moral integrity of sportsmen and sportswomen, especially young sportsmen and sportswomen.

2.   The Union and the Member States shall foster cooperation with third countries and the competent international organisations in the field of education and sport, in particular the Council of Europe.

3.   In order to contribute to the achievement of the objectives referred to in this Article:

(a)   European laws or framework laws shall establish incentive measures, excluding any harmonisation of the laws and regulations of the Member States. They shall be adopted after consultation of the Committee of the Regions and the Economic and Social Committee;

(b)   the Council, on a proposal from the Commission, shall adopt recommendations.

ARTICLE III-283

1.   The Union shall implement a vocational training policy which shall support and complement the action of the Member States, while fully respecting the responsibility of the Member States for the content and organisation of vocational training.

Union action shall aim to:

(a)   facilitate adaptation to industrial change, in particular through vocational training and retraining;

(b)   improve initial and continuing vocational training in order to facilitate vocational integration and reintegration into the labour market;

(c)   facilitate access to vocational training and encourage mobility of instructors and trainees and particularly young people;

(d)   stimulate cooperation on training between educational or training establishments and firms;

(e)   develop exchanges of information and experience on issues common to the training systems of the Member States.

2.   The Union and the Member States shall foster cooperation with third countries and the competent international organisations in the sphere of vocational training.

3.   In order to contribute to the achievement of the objectives referred to in this Article:

(a)   European laws or framework laws shall establish the necessary measures, excluding any harmonisation of the laws and regulations of the Member States. They shall be adopted after consultation of the Committee of the Regions and the Economic and Social Committee;

(b)   the Council, on a proposal from the Commission, shall adopt recommendations.

SECTION 6

CIVIL PROTECTION

ARTICLE III-284

1.   The Union shall encourage cooperation between Member States in order to improve the effectiveness of systems for preventing and protecting against natural or man-made disasters.

Union action shall aim to:

(a)   support and complement Member States' action at national, regional and local level in risk prevention, in preparing their civil-protection personnel and in responding to natural or man-made disasters within the Union;

(b)   promote swift, effective operational cooperation within the Union between national civil-protection services;

(c)   promote consistency in international civil-protection work.

2.   European laws or framework laws shall establish the measures necessary to help achieve the objectives referred to in paragraph 1, excluding any harmonisation of the laws and regulations of the Member States.

SECTION 7

ADMINISTRATIVE COOPERATION

ARTICLE III-285

1.   Effective implementation of Union law by the Member States, which is essential for the proper functioning of the Union, shall be regarded as a matter of common interest.

2.   The Union may support the efforts of Member States to improve their administrative capacity to implement Union law. Such action may include facilitating the exchange of information and of civil servants as well as supporting training schemes. No Member State shall be obliged to avail itself of such support. European laws shall establish the necessary measures to this end, excluding any harmonisation of the laws and regulations of the Member States.

3.   This Article shall be without prejudice to the obligations of the Member States to implement Union law or to the prerogatives and duties of the Commission. It shall also be without prejudice to other provisions of the Constitution providing for administrative cooperation among the Member States and between them and the Union.

TITLE IV

ASSOCIATION OF THE OVERSEAS COUNTRIES AND TERRITORIES

ARTICLE III-286

1.   The non-European countries and territories which have special relations with Denmark, France, the Netherlands and the United Kingdom shall be associated with the Union. These countries and territories, hereinafter called the "countries and territories", are listed in Annex II.

This title shall apply to Greenland, subject to the specific provisions of the Protocol on special arrangements for Greenland.

2.   The purpose of association shall be to promote the economic and social development of the countries and territories and to establish close economic relations between them and the Union.

Association shall serve primarily to further the interests and prosperity of the inhabitants of these countries and territories in order to lead them to the economic, social and cultural development to which they aspire.

ARTICLE III-287

Association shall have the following objectives:

(a)   Member States shall apply to their trade with the countries and territories the same treatment as they accord each other pursuant to the Constitution;

(b)   each country or territory shall apply to its trade with Member States and with the other countries and territories the same treatment as that which it applies to the European State with which it has special relations;

(c)   Member States shall contribute to the investments required for the progressive development of these countries and territories;

(d)   for investments financed by the Union, participation in tenders and supplies shall be open on equal terms to all natural and legal persons who are nationals of a Member State or of one of the countries and territories;

(e)   in relations between Member States and the countries and territories, the right of establishment of nationals and companies or firms shall be regulated in accordance with the provisions of Subsection 2 of Section 2 of Chapter I of Title III relating to the freedom of establishment and under the procedures laid down in that Subsection, and on a non-discriminatory basis, subject to any acts adopted pursuant to Article III-291.

ARTICLE III-288

1.   Customs duties on imports into the Member States of goods originating in the countries and territories shall be prohibited in conformity with the prohibition of customs duties between Member States provided for in the Constitution.

2.   Customs duties on imports into each country or territory from Member States or from the other countries or territories shall be prohibited in accordance with Article III-151(4).

3.   The countries and territories may, however, levy customs duties which meet the needs of their development and industrialisation or produce revenue for their budgets.

The duties referred to in the first subparagraph shall not exceed the level of those imposed on imports of products from the Member State with which each country or territory has special relations.

4.   Paragraph 2 shall not apply to countries and territories which, by reason of the particular international obligations by which they are bound, already apply a non-discriminatory customs tariff.

5.   The introduction of or any change in customs duties imposed on goods imported into the countries and territories shall not, either in law or in fact, give rise to any direct or indirect discrimination between imports from the various Member States.

ARTICLE III-289

If the level of the duties applicable to goods from a third country on entry into a country or territory is liable, when Article III-288(1) has been applied, to cause deflections of trade to the detriment of any Member State, the latter may request the Commission to propose to the other Member States that they take the necessary measures to remedy the situation.

ARTICLE III-290

Subject to the provisions relating to public health, public security or public policy, freedom of movement within Member States for workers from the countries and territories, and within the countries and territories for workers from Member States, shall be regulated by acts adopted in accordance with Article III-291.

ARTICLE III-291

The Council, on a proposal from the Commission, shall adopt unanimously, on the basis of the experience acquired under the association of the countries and territories with the Union, European laws, framework laws, regulations and decisions as regards the detailed rules and the procedure for the association of the countries and territories with the Union. These laws and framework laws shall be adopted after consultation of the European Parliament.

TITLE V

THE UNION'S EXTERNAL ACTION

CHAPTER I

PROVISIONS HAVING GENERAL APPLICATION

ARTICLE III-292

1. The Union's action on the international scene shall be guided by the principles which have inspired its own creation, development and enlargement, and which it seeks to advance in the wider world: democracy, the rule of law, the universality and indivisibility of human rights and fundamental freedoms, respect for human dignity, the principles of equality and solidarity, and respect for the principles of the United Nations Charter and international law.

The Union shall seek to develop relations and build partnerships with third countries, and international, regional or global organisations which share the principles referred to in the first subparagraph. It shall promote multilateral solutions to common problems, in particular in the framework of the United Nations.

2. The Union shall define and pursue common policies and actions, and shall work for a high degree of cooperation in all fields of international relations, in order to:

(a) safeguard its values, fundamental interests, security, independence and integrity;

(b) consolidate and support democracy, the rule of law, human rights and the principles of international law;

(c) preserve peace, prevent conflicts and strengthen international security, in accordance with the purposes and principles of the United Nations Charter, with the principles of the Helsinki Final Act and with the aims of the Charter of Paris, including those relating to external borders;

(d) foster the sustainable economic, social and environmental development of developing countries, with the primary aim of eradicating poverty;

(e) encourage the integration of all countries into the world economy, including through the progressive abolition of restrictions on international trade;

(f) help develop international measures to preserve and improve the quality of the environment and the sustainable management of global natural resources, in order to ensure sustainable development;

(g) assist populations, countries and regions confronting natural or man-made disasters;

(h) promote an international system based on stronger multilateral cooperation and good global governance.

3. The Union shall respect the principles and pursue the objectives set out in paragraphs 1 and 2 in the development and implementation of the different areas of the Union's external action covered by this Title and the external aspects of its other policies.

The Union shall ensure consistency between the different areas of its external action and between these and its other policies. The Council and the Commission, assisted by the Union Minister for Foreign Affairs, shall ensure that consistency and shall cooperate to that effect.

ARTICLE III-293

1.   On the basis of the principles and objectives set out in Article III-292, the European Council shall identify the strategic interests and objectives of the Union.

European decisions of the European Council on the strategic interests and objectives of the Union shall relate to the common foreign and security policy and to other areas of the external action of the Union. Such decisions may concern the relations of the Union with a specific country or region or may be thematic in approach. They shall define their duration, and the means to be made available by the Union and the Member States.

The European Council shall act unanimously on a recommendation from the Council, adopted by the latter under the arrangements laid down for each area. European decisions of the European Council shall be implemented in accordance with the procedures provided for in the Constitution.

2.   The Union Minister for Foreign Affairs, for the area of common foreign and security policy, and the Commission, for other areas of external action, may submit joint proposals to the Council.

CHAPTER II

COMMON FOREIGN AND SECURITY POLICY

SECTION 1

COMMON PROVISIONS

ARTICLE III-294

1.   In the context of the principles and objectives of its external action, the Union shall define and implement a common foreign and security policy covering all areas of foreign and security policy.

2.   The Member States shall support the common foreign and security policy actively and unreservedly in a spirit of loyalty and mutual solidarity.

The Member States shall work together to enhance and develop their mutual political solidarity. They shall refrain from any action which is contrary to the interests of the Union or likely to impair its effectiveness as a cohesive force in international relations.

The Council and the Union Minister for Foreign Affairs shall ensure that these principles are complied with.

3.   The Union shall conduct the common foreign and security policy by:

(a)   defining the general guidelines;

(b)   adopting European decisions defining:

   (i)   actions to be undertaken by the Union;

   (ii)   positions to be taken by the Union;

   (iii) arrangements for the implementation of the European decisions referred to in points (i) and (ii);

(c)   strengthening systematic cooperation between Member States in the conduct of policy.

ARTICLE III-295

1.   The European Council shall define the general guidelines for the common foreign and security policy, including for matters with defence implications.

If international developments so require, the President of the European Council shall convene an extraordinary meeting of the European Council in order to define the strategic lines of the Union's policy in the face of such developments.

2.   The Council shall adopt the European decisions necessary for defining and implementing the common foreign and security policy on the basis of the general guidelines and strategic lines defined by the European Council.

ARTICLE III-296

1.   The Union Minister for Foreign Affairs, who shall chair the Foreign Affairs Council, shall contribute through his or her proposals towards the preparation of the common foreign and security policy and shall ensure implementation of the European decisions adopted by the European Council and the Council.

2.   The Minister for Foreign Affairs shall represent the Union for matters relating to the common foreign and security policy. He or she shall conduct political dialogue with third parties on the Union's behalf and shall express the Union's position in international organisations and at international conferences.

3.   In fulfilling his or her mandate, the Union Minister for Foreign Affairs shall be assisted by a European External Action Service. This service shall work in cooperation with the diplomatic services of the Member States and shall comprise officials from relevant departments of the General Secretariat of the Council and of the Commission as well as staff seconded from national diplomatic services of the Member States. The organisation and functioning of the European External Action Service shall be established by a European decision of the Council. The Council shall act on a proposal from the Union Minister for Foreign Affairs after consulting the European Parliament and after obtaining the consent of the Commission.

ARTICLE III-297

1.   Where the international situation requires operational action by the Union, the Council shall adopt the necessary European decisions. Such decisions shall lay down the objectives, the scope, the means to be made available to the Union, if necessary the duration, and the conditions for implementation of the action.

If there is a change in circumstances having a substantial effect on a question subject to such a European decision, the Council shall review the principles and objectives of that decision and adopt the necessary European decisions.

2.   The European decisions referred to in paragraph 1 shall commit the Member States in the positions they adopt and in the conduct of their activity.

3.   Whenever there is any plan to adopt a national position or take national action pursuant to a European decision as referred to in paragraph 1, information shall be provided by the Member State concerned in time to allow, if necessary, for prior consultations within the Council. The obligation to provide prior information shall not apply to measures which are merely a national transposition of such a decision.

4.   In cases of imperative need arising from changes in the situation and failing a review of the European decision pursuant to the second subparagraph of paragraph 1, Member States may take the necessary measures as a matter of urgency, having regard to the general objectives of that decision. The Member State concerned shall inform the Council immediately of any such measures.

5.   Should there be any major difficulties in implementing a European decision as referred to in this Article, a Member State shall refer them to the Council which shall discuss them and seek appropriate solutions. Such solutions shall not run counter to the objectives of the action or impair its effectiveness.

ARTICLE III-298

The Council shall adopt European decisions which shall define the approach of the Union to a particular matter of a geographical or thematic nature. Member States shall ensure that their national policies conform to the positions of the Union.

ARTICLE III-299

1.   Any Member State, the Union Minister for Foreign Affairs, or that Minister with the Commission's support, may refer any question relating to the common foreign and security policy to the Council and may submit to it initiatives or proposals as appropriate.

2.   In cases requiring a rapid decision, the Union Minister for Foreign Affairs, of the Minister's own motion or at the request of a Member State, shall convene an extraordinary meeting of the Council within forty-eight hours or, in an emergency, within a shorter period.

ARTICLE III-300

1.   The European decisions referred to in this Chapter shall be adopted by the Council acting unanimously.

When abstaining in a vote, any member of the Council may qualify its abstention by making a formal declaration. In that case, it shall not be obliged to apply the European decision, but shall accept that the latter commits the Union. In a spirit of mutual solidarity, the Member State concerned shall refrain from any action likely to conflict with or impede Union action based on that decision and the other Member States shall respect its position. If the members of the Council qualifying their abstention in this way represent at least one third of the Member States comprising at least one third of the population of the Union, the decision shall not be adopted.

2.   By way of derogation from paragraph 1, the Council shall act by a qualified majority:

(a)   when adopting European decisions defining a Union action or position on the basis of a European decision of the European Council relating to the Union's strategic interests and objectives, as referred to in Article III-293(1);

(b)   when adopting a European decision defining a Union action or position, on a proposal which the Union Minister for Foreign Affairs has presented following a specific request to him or her from the European Council, made on its own initiative or that of the Minister;

(c)   when adopting a European decision implementing a European decision defining a Union action or position;

(d)   when adopting a European decision concerning the appointment of a special representative in accordance with Article III-302.

If a member of the Council declares that, for vital and stated reasons of national policy, it intends to oppose the adoption of a European decision to be adopted by a qualified majority, a vote shall not be taken. The Union Minister for Foreign Affairs will, in close consultation with the Member State involved, search for a solution acceptable to it. If he or she does not succeed, the Council may, acting by a qualified majority, request that the matter be referred to the European Council for a European decision by unanimity.

3.   In accordance with Article I-40(7) the European Council may unanimously adopt a European decision stipulating that the Council shall act by a qualified majority in cases other than those referred to in paragraph 2 of this Article.

4.   Paragraphs 2 and 3 shall not apply to decisions having military or defence implications.

ARTICLE III-301

1.   When the European Council or the Council has defined a common approach of the Union within the meaning of Article I-40(5), the Union Minister for Foreign Affairs and the Ministers for Foreign Affairs of the Member States shall coordinate their activities within the Council.

2.   The diplomatic missions of the Member States and the Union delegations in third countries and at international organisations shall cooperate and shall contribute to formulating and implementing the common approach referred to in paragraph 1.

ARTICLE III-302

The Council may appoint, on a proposal from the Union Minister for Foreign Affairs, a special representative with a mandate in relation to particular policy issues. The special representative shall carry out his or her mandate under the Minister's authority.

ARTICLE III-303

The Union may conclude agreements with one or more States or international organisations in areas covered by this Chapter.

ARTICLE III-304

1.   The Union Minister for Foreign Affairs shall consult and inform the European Parliament in accordance with Article I-40(8) and Article I-41(8). He or she shall ensure that the views of the European Parliament are duly taken into consideration. Special representatives may be involved in briefing the European Parliament.

2.   The European Parliament may ask questions of the Council and of the Union Minister for Foreign Affairs or make recommendations to them. Twice a year it shall hold a debate on progress in implementing the common foreign and security policy, including the common security and defence policy.

ARTICLE III-305

1.   Member States shall coordinate their action in international organisations and at international conferences. They shall uphold the Union's positions in such fora. The Union Minister for Foreign Affairs shall organise this coordination.

In international organisations and at international conferences where not all the Member States participate, those which do take part shall uphold the Union's positions.

2.   In accordance with Article I-16(2), Member States represented in international organisations or international conferences where not all the Member States participate shall keep the latter, as well as the Union Minister for Foreign Affairs, informed of any matter of common interest.

Member States which are also members of the United Nations Security Council shall concert and keep the other Member States and the Union Minister for Foreign Affairs fully informed. Member States which are members of the Security Council will, in the execution of their functions, defend the positions and the interests of the Union, without prejudice to their responsibilities under the United Nations Charter.

When the Union has defined a position on a subject which is on the United Nations Security Council agenda, those Member States which sit on the Security Council shall request that the Union Minister for Foreign Affairs be asked to present the Union's position.

ARTICLE III-306

The diplomatic and consular missions of the Member States and the Union delegations in third countries and international conferences, and their representations to international organisations, shall cooperate in ensuring that the European decisions defining Union positions and actions adopted pursuant to this Chapter are complied with and implemented. They shall step up cooperation by exchanging information and carrying out joint assessments.

They shall contribute to the implementation of the right of European citizens to protection in the territory of third countries as referred to in Article I-10(2)(c) and the measures adopted pursuant to Article III-127.

ARTICLE III-307

1.   Without prejudice to Article III-344, a Political and Security Committee shall monitor the international situation in the areas covered by the common foreign and security policy and contribute to the definition of policies by delivering opinions to the Council at the request of the latter, or of the Union Minister for Foreign Affairs, or on its own initiative. It shall also monitor the implementation of agreed policies, without prejudice to the powers of the Union Minister for Foreign Affairs.

2.   Within the scope of this Chapter, the Political and Security Committee shall exercise, under the responsibility of the Council and of the Union Minister for Foreign Affairs, the political control and strategic direction of the crisis management operations referred to in Article III-309.

The Council may authorise the Committee, for the purpose and for the duration of a crisis management operation, as determined by the Council, to take the relevant measures concerning the political control and strategic direction of the operation.

ARTICLE III-308

The implementation of the common foreign and security policy shall not affect the application of the procedures and the extent of the powers of the institutions laid down by the Constitution for the exercise of the Union competences referred to in Articles I-13 to I-15 and I-17.

Similarly, the implementation of the policies listed in those Articles shall not affect the application of the procedures and the extent of the powers of the institutions laid down by the Constitution for the exercise of the Union competences under this Chapter.

SECTION 2

THE COMMON SECURITY AND DEFENCE POLICY

ARTICLE III-309

1.   The tasks referred to in Article I-41(1), in the course of which the Union may use civilian and military means, shall include joint disarmament operations, humanitarian and rescue tasks, military advice and assistance tasks, conflict prevention and peace-keeping tasks, tasks of combat forces in crisis management, including peace-making and post-conflict stabilisation. All these tasks may contribute to the fight against terrorism, including by supporting third countries in combating terrorism in their territories.

2.   The Council shall adopt European decisions relating to the tasks referred to in paragraph 1, defining their objectives and scope and the general conditions for their implementation. The Union Minister for Foreign Affairs, acting under the authority of the Council and in close and constant contact with the Political and Security Committee, shall ensure coordination of the civilian and military aspects of such tasks.

ARTICLE III-310

1.   Within the framework of the European decisions adopted in accordance with Article III-309, the Council may entrust the implementation of a task to a group of Member States which are willing and have the necessary capability for such a task. Those Member States, in association with the Union Minister for Foreign Affairs, shall agree among themselves on the management of the task.

2.   Member States participating in the task shall keep the Council regularly informed of its progress on their own initiative or at the request of another Member State. Those States shall inform the Council immediately should the completion of the task entail major consequences or require amendment of the objective, scope and conditions determined for the task in the European decisions referred to in paragraph 1. In such cases, the Council shall adopt the necessary European decisions.

ARTICLE III-311

1.   The Agency in the field of defence capabilities development, research, acquisition and armaments (European Defence Agency), established by Article I-41(3) and subject to the authority of the Council, shall have as its task to:

(a)   contribute to identifying the Member States' military capability objectives and evaluating observance of the capability commitments given by the Member States;

(b)   promote harmonisation of operational needs and adoption of effective, compatible procurement methods;

(c)   propose multilateral projects to fulfil the objectives in terms of military capabilities, ensure coordination of the programmes implemented by the Member States and management of specific cooperation programmes;

(d)   support defence technology research, and coordinate and plan joint research activities and the study of technical solutions meeting future operational needs;

(e)   contribute to identifying and, if necessary, implementing any useful measure for strengthening the industrial and technological base of the defence sector and for improving the effectiveness of military expenditure.

2.   The European Defence Agency shall be open to all Member States wishing to be part of it. The Council, acting by a qualified majority, shall adopt a European decision defining the Agency's statute, seat and operational rules. That decision should take account of the level of effective participation in the Agency's activities. Specific groups shall be set up within the Agency bringing together Member States engaged in joint projects. The Agency shall carry out its tasks in liaison with the Commission where necessary.

ARTICLE III-312

1.   Those Member States which wish to participate in the permanent structured cooperation referred to in Article I-41(6), which fulfil the criteria and have made the commitments on military capabilities set out in the Protocol on permanent structured cooperation shall notify their intention to the Council and to the Union Minister for Foreign Affairs.

2.   Within three months following the notification referred to in paragraph 1 the Council shall adopt a European decision establishing permanent structured cooperation and determining the list of participating Member States. The Council shall act by a qualified majority after consulting the Union Minister for Foreign Affairs.

3.   Any Member State which, at a later stage, wishes to participate in the permanent structured cooperation shall notify its intention to the Council and to the Union Minister for Foreign Affairs.

The Council shall adopt a European decision confirming the participation of the Member State concerned which fulfils the criteria and makes the commitments referred to in Articles 1 and 2 of the Protocol on permanent structured cooperation. The Council shall act by a qualified majority after consulting the Union Minister for Foreign Affairs. Only members of the Council representing the participating Member States shall take part in the vote.

A qualified majority shall be defined as at least 55% of the members of the Council representing the participating Member States, comprising at least 65% of the population of these States.

A blocking minority must include at least the minimum number of Council members representing more than 35% of the population of the participating Member States, plus one member, failing which the qualified majority shall be deemed attained.

4.   If a participating Member State no longer fulfils the criteria or is no longer able to meet the commitments referred to in Articles 1 and 2 of the Protocol on permanent structured cooperation, the Council may adopt a European decision suspending the participation of the Member State concerned.

The Council shall act by a qualified majority. Only members of the Council representing the participating Member States, with the exception of the Member State in question, shall take part in the vote.

A qualified majority shall be defined as at least 55% of the members of the Council representing the participating Member States, comprising at least 65% of the population of these States.

A blocking minority must include at least the minimum number of Council members representing more than 35% of the population of the participating Member States, plus one member, failing which the qualified majority shall be deemed attained.

5.   Any participating Member State which wishes to withdraw from permanent structured cooperation shall notify its intention to the Council, which shall take note that the Member State in question has ceased to participate.

6.   The European decisions and recommendations of the Council within the framework of permanent structured cooperation, other than those provided for in paragraphs 2 to 5, shall be adopted by unanimity. For the purposes of this paragraph, unanimity shall be constituted by the votes of the representatives of the participating Member States only.

SECTION 3

FINANCIAL PROVISIONS

ARTICLE III-313

1.   Administrative expenditure which the implementation of this Chapter entails for the institutions shall be charged to the Union budget.

2.   Operating expenditure to which the implementation of this Chapter gives rise shall also be charged to the Union budget, except for such expenditure arising from operations having military or defence implications and cases where the Council decides otherwise.

In cases where expenditure is not charged to the Union budget it shall be charged to the Member States in accordance with the gross national product scale, unless the Council decides otherwise. As for expenditure arising from operations having military or defence implications, Member States whose representatives in the Council have made a formal declaration under Article III-300(1), second subparagraph, shall not be obliged to contribute to the financing thereof.

3.   The Council shall adopt a European decision establishing the specific procedures for guaranteeing rapid access to appropriations in the Union budget for urgent financing of initiatives in the framework of the common foreign and security policy, and in particular for preparatory activities for the tasks referred to in Article I-41(1) and Article III-309. It shall act after consulting the European Parliament.

Preparatory activities for the tasks referred to in Article I-41(1) and Article III-309 which are not charged to the Union budget shall be financed by a start-up fund made up of Member States' contributions.

The Council shall adopt by a qualified majority, on a proposal from the Union Minister for Foreign Affairs, European decisions establishing:

(a)   the procedures for setting up and financing the start-up fund, in particular the amounts allocated to the fund;

(b)   the procedures for administering the start-up fund;

(c)   the financial control procedures.

When the task planned in accordance with Article I-41(1) and Article III-309 cannot be charged to the Union budget, the Council shall authorise the Union Minister for Foreign Affairs to use the fund. The Union Minister for Foreign Affairs shall report to the Council on the implementation of this remit.

CHAPTER III

COMMON COMMERCIAL POLICY

ARTICLE III-314

By establishing a customs union in accordance with Article III-151, the Union shall contribute, in the common interest, to the harmonious development of world trade, the progressive abolition of restrictions on international trade and on foreign direct investment, and the lowering of customs and other barriers.

ARTICLE III-315

1.   The common commercial policy shall be based on uniform principles, particularly with regard to changes in tariff rates, the conclusion of tariff and trade agreements relating to trade in goods and services, and the commercial aspects of intellectual property, foreign direct investment, the achievement of uniformity in measures of liberalisation, export policy and measures to protect trade such as those to be taken in the event of dumping or subsidies. The common commercial policy shall be conducted in the context of the principles and objectives of the Union's external action.

2.   European laws shall establish the measures defining the framework for implementing the common commercial policy.

3.   Where agreements with one or more third countries or international organisations need to be negotiated and concluded, Article III-325 shall apply, subject to the special provisions of this Article.

The Commission shall make recommendations to the Council, which shall authorise it to open the necessary negotiations. The Council and the Commission shall be responsible for ensuring that the agreements negotiated are compatible with internal Union policies and rules.

The Commission shall conduct these negotiations in consultation with a special committee appointed by the Council to assist the Commission in this task and within the framework of such directives as the Council may issue to it. The Commission shall report regularly to the special committee and to the European Parliament on the progress of negotiations.

4.   For the negotiation and conclusion of the agreements referred to in paragraph 3, the Council shall act by a qualified majority.

For the negotiation and conclusion of agreements in the fields of trade in services and the commercial aspects of intellectual property, as well as foreign direct investment, the Council shall act unanimously where such agreements include provisions for which unanimity is required for the adoption of internal rules.

The Council shall also act unanimously for the negotiation and conclusion of agreements:

(a)   in the field of trade in cultural and audiovisual services, where these agreements risk prejudicing the Union's cultural and linguistic diversity;

(b)   in the field of trade in social, education and health services, where these agreements risk seriously disturbing the national organisation of such services and prejudicing the responsibility of Member States to deliver them.

5.   The negotiation and conclusion of international agreements in the field of transport shall be subject to Section 7 of Chapter III of Title III and to Article III-325.

6.   The exercise of the competences conferred by this Article in the field of the common commercial policy shall not affect the delimitation of competences between the Union and the Member States, and shall not lead to harmonisation of legislative or regulatory provisions of the Member States insofar as the Constitution excludes such harmonisation.

CHAPTER IV

COOPERATION WITH THIRD COUNTRIES AND HUMANITARIAN AID

SECTION 1

DEVELOPMENT COOPERATION

ARTICLE III-316

1.   Union policy in the field of development cooperation shall be conducted within the framework of the principles and objectives of the Union's external action. The Union's development cooperation policy and that of the Member States shall complement and reinforce each other.

Union development cooperation policy shall have as its primary objective the reduction and, in the long term, the eradication of poverty. The Union shall take account of the objectives of development cooperation in the policies that it implements which are likely to affect developing countries.

2.   The Union and the Member States shall comply with the commitments and take account of the objectives they have approved in the context of the United Nations and other competent international organisations.

ARTICLE III-317

1.   European laws or framework laws shall establish the measures necessary for the implementation of development cooperation policy, which may relate to multiannual cooperation programmes with developing countries or programmes with a thematic approach.

2.   The Union may conclude with third countries and competent international organisations any agreement helping to achieve the objectives referred to in Articles III-292 and III-316.

The first subparagraph shall be without prejudice to Member States' competence to negotiate in international bodies and to conclude agreements.

3.   The European Investment Bank shall contribute, under the terms laid down in its Statute, to the implementation of the measures referred to in paragraph 1.

ARTICLE III-318

1.   In order to promote the complementarity and efficiency of their action, the Union and the Member States shall coordinate their policies on development cooperation and shall consult each other on their aid programmes, including in international organisations and during international conferences. They may undertake joint action. Member States shall contribute if necessary to the implementation of Union aid programmes.

2.   The Commission may take any useful initiative to promote the coordination referred to in paragraph 1.

3.   Within their respective spheres of competence, the Union and the Member States shall cooperate with third countries and the competent international organisations.

SECTION 2

ECONOMIC, FINANCIAL AND TECHNICAL COOPERATION WITH THIRD COUNTRIES

ARTICLE III-319

1.   Without prejudice to the other provisions of the Constitution, and in particular Articles III-316 to III-318, the Union shall carry out economic, financial and technical cooperation measures, including assistance, in particular financial assistance, with third countries other than developing countries. Such measures shall be consistent with the development policy of the Union and shall be carried out within the framework of the principles and objectives of its external action. The Union's measures and those of the Member States shall complement and reinforce each other.

2.   European laws or framework laws shall establish the measures necessary for the implementation of paragraph 1.

3.   Within their respective spheres of competence, the Union and the Member States shall cooperate with third countries and the competent international organisations. The arrangements for Union cooperation may be the subject of agreements between the Union and the third parties concerned.

The first subparagraph shall be without prejudice to Member States' competence to negotiate in international bodies and to conclude agreements.

ARTICLE III-320

When the situation in a third country requires urgent financial assistance from the Union, the Council shall adopt the necessary European decisions on a proposal from the Commission.

SECTION 3

HUMANITARIAN AID

ARTICLE III-321

1.   The Union's operations in the field of humanitarian aid shall be conducted within the framework of the principles and objectives of the external action of the Union. Such operations shall be intended to provide ad hoc assistance and relief and protection for people in third countries who are victims of natural or man-made disasters, in order to meet the humanitarian needs resulting from these different situations. The Union's operations and those of the Member States shall complement and reinforce each other.

2.   Humanitarian aid operations shall be conducted in compliance with the principles of international law and with the principles of impartiality, neutrality and non-discrimination.

3.   European laws or framework laws shall establish the measures defining the framework within which the Union's humanitarian aid operations shall be implemented.

4.   The Union may conclude with third countries and competent international organisations any agreement helping to achieve the objectives referred to in paragraph 1 and in Article III-292.

The first subparagraph shall be without prejudice to Member States' competence to negotiate in international bodies and to conclude agreements.

5.   In order to establish a framework for joint contributions from young Europeans to the humanitarian aid operations of the Union, a European Voluntary Humanitarian Aid Corps shall be set up. European laws shall determine the rules and procedures for the operation of the Corps.

6. The Commission may take any useful initiative to promote coordination between actions of the Union and those of the Member States, in order to enhance the efficiency and complementarity of Union and national humanitarian aid measures.

7. The Union shall ensure that its humanitarian aid operations are coordinated and consistent with those of international organisations and bodies, in particular those forming part of the United Nations system.

CHAPTER V

RESTRICTIVE MEASURES

ARTICLE III-322

1. Where a European decision, adopted in accordance with Chapter II, provides for the interruption or reduction, in part or completely, of economic and financial relations with one or more third countries, the Council, acting by a qualified majority on a joint proposal from the Union Minister for Foreign Affairs and the Commission, shall adopt the necessary European regulations or decisions. It shall inform the European Parliament thereof.

2. Where a European decision adopted in accordance with Chapter II so provides, the Council may adopt restrictive measures under the procedure referred to in paragraph 1 against natural or legal persons and groups or non-State entities.

3. The acts referred to in this Article shall include necessary provisions on legal safeguards.

CHAPTER VI

INTERNATIONAL AGREEMENTS

ARTICLE III-323

1. The Union may conclude an agreement with one or more third countries or international organisations where the Constitution so provides or where the conclusion of an agreement is necessary in order to achieve, within the framework of the Union's policies, one of the objectives referred to in the Constitution, or is provided for in a legally binding Union act or is likely to affect common rules or alter their scope.

2. Agreements concluded by the Union are binding on the institutions of the Union and on its Member States.

ARTICLE III-324

The Union may conclude an association agreement with one or more third countries or international organisations in order to establish an association involving reciprocal rights and obligations, common actions and special procedures.

ARTICLE III-325

1.   Without prejudice to the specific provisions laid down in Article III-315, agreements between the Union and third countries or international organisations shall be negotiated and concluded in accordance with the following procedure.

2.   The Council shall authorise the opening of negotiations, adopt negotiating directives, authorise the signing of agreements and conclude them.

3.   The Commission, or the Union Minister for Foreign Affairs where the agreement envisaged relates exclusively or principally to the common foreign and security policy, shall submit recommendations to the Council, which shall adopt a European decision authorising the opening of negotiations and, depending on the subject of the agreement envisaged, nominating the Union negotiator or head of the Union's negotiating team.

4.   The Council may address directives to the negotiator and designate a special committee in consultation with which the negotiations must be conducted.

5.   The Council, on a proposal by the negotiator, shall adopt a European decision authorising the signing of the agreement and, if necessary, its provisional application before entry into force.

6.   The Council, on a proposal by the negotiator, shall adopt a European decision concluding the agreement.

Except where agreements relate exclusively to the common foreign and security policy, the Council shall adopt the European decision concluding the agreement:

(a)   after obtaining the consent of the European Parliament in the following cases:

    (i)   association agreements;

    (ii)   Union accession to the European Convention for the Protection of Human Rights and Fundamental Freedoms;

    (iii)   agreements establishing a specific institutional framework by organising cooperation procedures;

    (iv)   agreements with important budgetary implications for the Union;

    (v)   agreements covering fields to which either the ordinary legislative procedure applies, or the special legislative procedure where consent by the European Parliament is required.

The European Parliament and the Council may, in an urgent situation, agree upon a time-limit for consent.

(b)   after consulting the European Parliament in other cases. The European Parliament shall deliver its opinion within a time-limit which the Council may set depending on the urgency of the matter. In the absence of an opinion within that time-limit, the Council may act.

7.   When concluding an agreement, the Council may, by way of derogation from paragraphs 5, 6 and 9, authorise the negotiator to approve on the Union's behalf modifications to the agreement where it provides for them to be adopted by a simplified procedure or by a body set up by the agreement. The Council may attach specific conditions to such authorisation.

8.   The Council shall act by a qualified majority throughout the procedure.

However, it shall act unanimously when the agreement covers a field for which unanimity is required for the adoption of a Union act as well as for association agreements and the agreements referred to in Article III-319 with the States which are candidates for accession.

9.   The Council, on a proposal from the Commission or the Union Minister for Foreign Affairs, shall adopt a European decision suspending application of an agreement and establishing the positions to be adopted on the Union's behalf in a body set up by an agreement, when that body is called upon to adopt acts having legal effects, with the exception of acts supplementing or amending the institutional framework of the agreement.

10.   The European Parliament shall be immediately and fully informed at all stages of the procedure.

11.   A Member State, the European Parliament, the Council or the Commission may obtain the opinion of the Court of Justice as to whether an agreement envisaged is compatible with the Constitution. Where the opinion of the Court of Justice is adverse, the agreement envisaged may not enter into force unless it is amended or the Constitution is revised.

ARTICLE III-326

1.   By way of derogation from Article III-325, the Council, either on a recommendation from the European Central Bank or on a recommendation from the Commission and after consulting the European Central Bank, in an endeavour to reach a consensus consistent with the objective of price stability, may conclude formal agreements on an exchange-rate system for the euro in relation to the currencies of third States. The Council shall act unanimously after consulting the European Parliament and in accordance with the procedure provided for in paragraph 3.

The Council, either on a recommendation from the European Central Bank or on a recommendation from the Commission and after consulting the European Central Bank, in an endeavour to reach a consensus consistent with the objective of price stability, may adopt, adjust or abandon the central rates of the euro within the exchange-rate system. The President of the Council shall inform the European Parliament of the adoption, adjustment or abandonment of the central rates of the euro.

2.   In the absence of an exchange-rate system in relation to one or more currencies of third States as referred to in paragraph 1, the Council, acting either on a recommendation from the European Central Bank or on a recommendation from the Commission and after consulting

the European Central Bank, may formulate general orientations for exchange-rate policy in relation to these currencies. These general orientations shall be without prejudice to the primary objective of the European System of Central Banks, to maintain price stability.

3.   By way of derogation from Article III-325, where agreements on matters relating to the monetary or exchange-rate system are to be the subject of negotiations between the Union and one or more third States or international organisations, the Council, acting on a recommendation from the Commission and after consulting the European Central Bank, shall decide the arrangements for the negotiation and for the conclusion of such agreements. These arrangements shall ensure that the Union expresses a single position. The Commission shall be fully associated with the negotiations.

4.   Without prejudice to Union competence and Union agreements as regards economic and monetary union, Member States may negotiate in international bodies and conclude agreements.

CHAPTER VII

THE UNION'S RELATIONS WITH INTERNATIONAL ORGANISATIONS

AND THIRD COUNTRIES AND UNION DELEGATIONS

ARTICLE III-327

1.   The Union shall establish all appropriate forms of cooperation with the organs of the United Nations and its specialised agencies, the Council of Europe, the Organisation for Security and Cooperation in Europe and the Organisation for Economic Cooperation and Development.

The Union shall also maintain such relations as are appropriate with other international organisations.

2.   The Union Minister for Foreign Affairs and the Commission shall be instructed to implement this Article.

ARTICLE III-328

1.   Union delegations in third countries and at international organisations shall represent the Union.

2.   Union delegations shall be placed under the authority of the Union Minister for Foreign Affairs. They shall act in close cooperation with Member States' diplomatic and consular missions.

CHAPTER VIII

IMPLEMENTATION OF THE SOLIDARITY CLAUSE

ARTICLE III-329

1.   Should a Member State be the object of a terrorist attack or the victim of a natural or man-made disaster, the other Member States shall assist it at the request of its political authorities. To that end, the Member States shall coordinate between themselves in the Council.

2.   The arrangements for the implementation by the Union of the solidarity clause referred to in Article I-43 shall be defined by a European decision adopted by the Council acting on a joint proposal by the Commission and the Union Minister for Foreign Affairs. The Council shall act in accordance with Article III-300(1) where this decision has defence implications. The European Parliament shall be informed.

For the purposes of this paragraph and without prejudice to Article III-344, the Council shall be assisted by the Political and Security Committee with the support of the structures developed in the context of the common security and defence policy and by the Committee referred to in Article III-261; the two committees shall, if necessary, submit joint opinions.

3.   The European Council shall regularly assess the threats facing the Union in order to enable the Union and its Member States to take effective action.

TITLE VI

THE FUNCTIONING OF THE UNION

CHAPTER I

PROVISIONS GOVERNING THE INSTITUTIONS

SECTION 1

THE INSTITUTIONS

Subsection 1
The European Parliament

ARTICLE III-330

1.   A European law or framework law of the Council shall establish the necessary measures for the election of the Members of the European Parliament by direct universal suffrage in accordance with a uniform procedure in all Member States or in accordance with principles common to all Member States.

The Council shall act unanimously on initiative from, and after obtaining the consent of, the European Parliament, which shall act by a majority of its component members. This law or framework law shall enter into force after it has been approved by the Member States in accordance with their respective constitutional requirements.

2.   A European law of the European Parliament shall lay down the regulations and general conditions governing the performance of the duties of its Members. The European Parliament shall act on its own initiative after seeking an opinion from the Commission and after obtaining the consent of the Council. The Council shall act unanimously on all rules or conditions relating to the taxation of Members or former Members.

ARTICLE III-331

European laws shall lay down the regulations governing the political parties at European level referred to in Article I-46(4), and in particular the rules regarding their funding.

ARTICLE III-332

The European Parliament may, by a majority of its component Members, request the Commission to submit any appropriate proposal on matters on which it considers that a Union act is required for the purpose of implementing the Constitution. If the Commission does not submit a proposal, it shall inform the European Parliament of the reasons.

ARTICLE III-333

In the course of its duties, the European Parliament may, at the request of a quarter of its component Members, set up a temporary Committee of Inquiry to investigate, without prejudice to the powers conferred by the Constitution on other institutions or bodies, alleged contraventions or maladministration in the implementation of Union law, except where the alleged facts are being examined before a court and while the case is still subject to legal proceedings.

The temporary Committee of Inquiry shall cease to exist on submission of its report.

A European law of the European Parliament shall lay down the detailed provisions governing the exercise of the right of inquiry. The European Parliament shall act on its own initiative after obtaining the consent of the Council and of the Commission.

ARTICLE III-334

In accordance with Article I-10(2)(d), any citizen of the Union, and any natural or legal person residing or having its registered office in a Member State, shall have the right to address, individually or in association with other persons, a petition to the European Parliament on a matter which comes within the Union's fields of activity and which affects him, her or it directly.

ARTICLE III-335

1.   The European Parliament shall elect a European Ombudsman. In accordance with Articles I-10(2)(d) and I-49, he or she shall be empowered to receive complaints from any citizen of the Union or any natural or legal person residing or having its registered office in a Member State concerning instances of maladministration in the activities of the Union's institutions, bodies, offices or agencies, with the exception of the Court of Justice of the European Union acting in its judicial role.

In accordance with his or her duties, the Ombudsman shall conduct inquiries for which he or she finds grounds, either on his or her own initiative or on the basis of complaints submitted to him or her direct or through a member of the European Parliament, except where the alleged facts are or have been the subject of legal proceedings. Where the Ombudsman establishes an instance of maladministration, he or she shall refer the matter to the institution, body, office or agency concerned, which shall have a period of three months in which to inform him or her of its views. The European Ombudsman shall then forward a report to the European Parliament and the institution, body, office or agency concerned. The person lodging the complaint shall be informed of the outcome of such inquiries.

The Ombudsman shall submit an annual report to the European Parliament on the outcome of his or her inquiries.

2.   The Ombudsman shall be elected after each election of the European Parliament for the duration of its term of office. The Ombudsman shall be eligible for reappointment.

The Ombudsman may be dismissed by the Court of Justice at the request of the European Parliament if he or she no longer fulfils the conditions required for the performance of his or her duties or if he or she is guilty of serious misconduct.

3.   The Ombudsman shall be completely independent in the performance of his or her duties. In the performance of those duties he or she shall neither seek nor take instructions from any institution, body, office or agency. The Ombudsman shall not, during his or her term of office, engage in any other occupation, whether gainful or not.

4.   A European law of the European Parliament shall lay down the regulations and general conditions governing the performance of the Ombudsman's duties. The European Parliament shall act on its own initiative after seeking an opinion from the Commission and after obtaining the consent of the Council.

ARTICLE III-336

The European Parliament shall hold an annual session. It shall meet, without requiring to be convened, on the second Tuesday in March.

The European Parliament may meet in extraordinary part-session at the request of a majority of its component members or at the request of the Council or of the Commission.

ARTICLE III-337

1.   The European Council and the Council shall be heard by the European Parliament in accordance with the conditions laid down in the Rules of Procedure of the European Council and those of the Council.

2.   The Commission may attend all the meetings of the European Parliament and shall, at its request, be heard. It shall reply orally or in writing to questions put to it by the European Parliament or by its members.

3.   The European Parliament shall discuss in open session the annual general report submitted to it by the Commission.

ARTICLE III-338

Save as otherwise provided in the Constitution, the European Parliament shall act by a majority of the votes cast. Its Rules of Procedure shall determine the quorum.

ARTICLE III-339

The European Parliament shall adopt its Rules of Procedure, by a majority of its component members.

The proceedings of the European Parliament shall be published in the manner laid down in the Constitution and the Rules of Procedure of the European Parliament.

ARTICLE III-340

If a motion of censure on the activities of the Commission is tabled before it, the European Parliament shall not vote thereon until at least three days after the motion has been tabled and shall do so only by open vote.

If the motion of censure is carried by a two-thirds majority of the votes cast, representing a majority of the component members of the European Parliament, the members of the Commission shall resign as a body and the Union Minister for Foreign Affairs shall resign from duties that he or she carries out in the Commission. They shall remain in office and continue to deal with current business until they are replaced in accordance with Articles I-26 and I-27. In this case, the term of office of the members of the Commission appointed to replace them shall expire on the date on which the term of office of the members of the Commission obliged to resign as a body would have expired.

Subsection 2

The European Council

ARTICLE III-341

1.   Where a vote is taken, any member of the European Council may also act on behalf of not more than one other member.

Abstentions by members present in person or represented shall not prevent the adoption by the European Council of acts which require unanimity.

2.   The President of the European Parliament may be invited to be heard by the European Council.

3.   The European Council shall act by a simple majority for procedural questions and for the adoption of its Rules of Procedure.

4.   The European Council shall be assisted by the General Secretariat of the Council.

Subsection 3

The Council of Ministers

ARTICLE III-342

The Council shall meet when convened by its President on his or her own initiative, or at the request of one of its members or of the Commission.

ARTICLE III-343

1.   Where a vote is taken, any member of the Council may act on behalf of not more than one other member.

2.   Where it is required to act by a simple majority, the Council shall act by a majority of its component members.

3.   Abstentions by members present in person or represented shall not prevent the adoption by the Council of acts which require unanimity.

ARTICLE III-344

1.   A committee consisting of the Permanent Representatives of the Governments of the Member States shall be responsible for preparing the work of the Council and for carrying out the tasks assigned to it by the latter. The Committee may adopt procedural decisions in cases provided for in the Council's Rules of Procedure.

2.   The Council shall be assisted by a General Secretariat, under the responsibility of a Secretary-General appointed by the Council .

The Council shall decide on the organisation of the General Secretariat by a simple majority.

3.   The Council shall act by a simple majority regarding procedural matters and for the adoption of its Rules of Procedure.

ARTICLE III-345

The Council, by a simple majority, may request the Commission to undertake any studies the Council considers desirable for the attainment of the common objectives, and to submit any appropriate proposals to it. If the Commission does not submit a proposal, it shall inform the Council of the reasons.

ARTICLE III-346

The Council shall adopt European decisions laying down the rules governing the committees provided for in the Constitution. It shall act by a simple majority after consulting the Commission.

Subsection 4

The European Commission

ARTICLE III-347

The members of the Commission shall refrain from any action incompatible with their duties. Member States shall respect their independence and shall not seek to influence them in the performance of their tasks.

The members of the Commission shall not, during their term of office, engage in any other occupation, whether gainful or not. When entering upon their duties they shall give a solemn undertaking that, both during and after their term of office, they will respect the obligations arising therefrom and in particular their duty to behave with integrity and discretion as regards the acceptance, after they have ceased to hold office, of certain appointments or benefits. In the event of any breach of these obligations, the Court of Justice may, on application by the Council, acting by a simple majority, or the Commission, rule that the person concerned be, according to the circumstances, either compulsorily retired in accordance with Article III-349 or deprived of his or her right to a pension or other benefits in its stead.

ARTICLE III-348

1.   Apart from normal replacement, or death, the duties of a member of the Commission shall end when he or she resigns or is compulsorily retired.

2.   A vacancy caused by resignation, compulsory retirement or death shall be filled for the remainder of the member's term of office by a new member of the same nationality appointed

by the Council, by common accord with the President of the Commission, after consulting the European Parliament and in accordance with the criteria set out in Article I-26(4).

The Council may, acting unanimously on a proposal from the President of the Commission, decide that such a vacancy need not be filled, in particular when the remainder of the member's term of office is short.

3.   In the event of resignation, compulsory retirement or death, the President shall be replaced for the remainder of his or her term of office in accordance with Article I-27(1).

4.   In the event of resignation, compulsory retirement or death, the Union Minister for Foreign Affairs shall be replaced, for the remainder of his or her term of office, in accordance with Article I-28(1).

5.   In the case of the resignation of all the members of the Commission, they shall remain in office and continue to deal with current business until they have been replaced, for the remainder of their term of office, in accordance with Articles I-26 and I-27.

ARTICLE III-349

If any member of the Commission no longer fulfils the conditions required for the performance of his or her duties or if he or she has been guilty of serious misconduct, the Court of Justice may, on application by the Council, acting by a simple majority, or by the Commission, compulsorily retire him or her.

ARTICLE III-350

Without prejudice to Article I-28(4), the responsibilities incumbent upon the Commission shall be structured and allocated among its members by its President, in accordance with Article I-27(3). The President may reshuffle the allocation of those responsibilities during the Commission's term of office. The members of the Commission shall carry out the duties devolved upon them by the President under his or her authority.

ARTICLE III-351

The Commission shall act by a majority of its members. Its Rules of Procedure shall determine the quorum.

ARTICLE III-352

1.   The Commission shall adopt its Rules of Procedure so as to ensure both its own operation and that of its departments. It shall ensure that these rules are published.

2.   The Commission shall publish annually, not later than one month before the opening of the session of the European Parliament, a general report on the activities of the Union.

Subsection 5

The Court of Justice of the European Union

ARTICLE III-353

The Court of Justice shall sit in chambers, as a Grand Chamber or as a full Court, in accordance with the Statute of the Court of Justice of the European Union.

ARTICLE III-354

The Court of Justice shall be assisted by eight Advocates-General. Should the Court of Justice so request, the Council may, acting unanimously, adopt a European decision to increase the number of Advocates-General.

It shall be the duty of the Advocate-General, acting with complete impartiality and independence, to make, in open court, reasoned submissions on cases which, in accordance with the Statute of the Court of Justice of the European Union, require his or her involvement.

ARTICLE III-355

The Judges and Advocates-General of the Court of Justice shall be chosen from persons whose independence is beyond doubt and who possess the qualifications required for appointment to the highest judicial offices in their respective countries or who are jurisconsults of recognised competence; they shall be appointed by common accord of the governments of the Member States after consultation of the panel provided for in Article III-357.

Every three years there shall be a partial replacement of the Judges and Advocates-General, in accordance with the conditions laid down in the Statute of the Court of Justice of the European Union.

The Judges shall elect the President of the Court of Justice from among their number for a term of three years. He or she may be re-elected.

The Court of Justice shall adopt its Rules of Procedure. Those Rules shall require the consent of the Council.

ARTICLE III-356

The number of Judges of the General Court shall be determined by the Statute of the Court of Justice of the European Union. The Statute may provide for the General Court to be assisted by Advocates-General.

The members of the General Court shall be chosen from persons whose independence is beyond doubt and who possess the ability required for appointment to high judicial office. They shall be appointed by common accord of the governments of the Member States after consultation of the panel provided for in Article III-357.

The membership of the General Court shall be partially renewed every three years.

The Judges shall elect the President of the General Court from among their number for a term of three years. He or she may be re-elected.

The General Court shall establish its Rules of Procedure in agreement with the Court of Justice. The Rules shall be subject to the consent of the Council.

Unless the Statute provides otherwise, the provisions of the Constitution relating to the Court of Justice shall apply to the General Court.

ARTICLE III-357

A panel shall be set up in order to give an opinion on candidates' suitability to perform the duties of Judge and Advocate-General of the Court of Justice and the General Court before the governments of the Member States make the appointments referred to in Articles III-355 and III-356.

The panel shall comprise seven persons chosen from among former members of the Court of Justice and the General Court, members of national supreme courts and lawyers of recognised competence, one of whom shall be proposed by the European Parliament. The Council shall adopt a European decision establishing the panel's operating rules and a European decision appointing its members. It shall act on the initiative of the President of the Court of Justice.

ARTICLE III-358

1.   The General Court shall have jurisdiction to hear and determine at first instance actions or proceedings referred to in Articles III-365, III-367, III-370, III-372 and III-374, with the exception of those assigned to a specialised court set up under Article III-359 and those reserved in the Statute of the Court of Justice of the European Union for the Court of Justice. The Statute may provide for the General Court to have jurisdiction for other classes of action or proceeding.

Decisions given by the General Court under this paragraph may be subject to a right of appeal to the Court of Justice on points of law only, under the conditions and within the limits laid down by the Statute.

2.   The General Court shall have jurisdiction to hear and determine actions or proceedings brought against decisions of the specialised courts.

Decisions given by the General Court under this paragraph may exceptionally be subject to review by the Court of Justice, under the conditions and within the limits laid down by the Statute of the Court of Justice of the European Union, where there is a serious risk of the unity or consistency of Union law being affected.

3.   The General Court shall have jurisdiction to hear and determine questions referred for a preliminary ruling under Article III-369, in specific areas laid down by the Statute of the Court of Justice of the European Union.

Where the General Court considers that the case requires a decision of principle likely to affect the unity or consistency of Union law, it may refer the case to the Court of Justice for a ruling.

Decisions given by the General Court on questions referred for a preliminary ruling may exceptionally be subject to review by the Court of Justice, under the conditions and within the limits laid down by the Statute, where there is a serious risk of the unity or consistency of Union law being affected.

ARTICLE III-359

1.   European laws may establish specialised courts attached to the General Court to hear and determine at first instance certain classes of action or proceeding brought in specific areas. They shall be adopted either on a proposal from the Commission after consultation of the Court of Justice or at the request of the Court of Justice after consultation of the Commission.

2.   The European law establishing a specialised court shall lay down the rules on the organisation of the court and the extent of the jurisdiction conferred upon it.

3.   Decisions given by specialised courts may be subject to a right of appeal on points of law only or, when provided for in the European law establishing the specialised court, a right of appeal also on matters of fact, before the General Court.

4.   The members of the specialised courts shall be chosen from persons whose independence is beyond doubt and who possess the ability required for appointment to judicial office. They shall be appointed by the Council, acting unanimously.

5.   The specialised courts shall establish their Rules of Procedure in agreement with the Court of Justice. Those Rules shall require the consent of the Council.

6.   Unless the European law establishing the specialised court provides otherwise, the provisions of the Constitution relating to the Court of Justice of the European Union and the provisions of the Statute of the Court of Justice of the European Union shall apply to the specialised courts. Title I of the Statute and Article 64 thereof shall in any case apply to the specialised courts.

ARTICLE III-360

If the Commission considers that a Member State has failed to fulfil an obligation under the Constitution, it shall deliver a reasoned opinion on the matter after giving the State concerned the opportunity to submit its observations.

If the State concerned does not comply with the opinion within the period laid down by the Commission, the latter may bring the matter before the Court of Justice of the European Union.

ARTICLE III-361

A Member State which considers that another Member State has failed to fulfil an obligation under the Constitution may bring the matter before the Court of Justice of the European Union.

Before a Member State brings an action against another Member State for an alleged infringement of an obligation under the Constitution, it shall bring the matter before the Commission.

The Commission shall deliver a reasoned opinion after each of the States concerned has been given the opportunity to submit its own case and its observations on the other party's case both orally and in writing.

If the Commission has not delivered an opinion within three months of the date on which the matter was brought before it, the absence of such opinion shall not prevent the matter from being brought before the Court.

ARTICLE III-362

1.   If the Court of Justice of the European Union finds that a Member State has failed to fulfil an obligation under the Constitution, that State shall be required to take the necessary measures to comply with the judgment of the Court.

2.   If the Commission considers that the Member State concerned has not taken the necessary measures to comply with the judgment referred to in paragraph 1, it may bring the case before the Court of Justice of the European Union after giving that State the opportunity to submit its observations. It shall specify the amount of the lump sum or penalty payment to be paid by the Member State concerned which it considers appropriate in the circumstances.

If the Court finds that the Member State concerned has not complied with its judgment it may impose a lump sum or penalty payment on it.

This procedure shall be without prejudice to Article III-361.

3.   When the Commission brings a case before the Court of Justice of the European Union pursuant to Article III-360 on the grounds that the Member State concerned has failed to fulfil its obligation to notify measures transposing a European framework law, it may, when it deems appropriate, specify the amount of the lump sum or penalty payment to be paid by the Member State concerned which it considers appropriate in the circumstances.

If the Court finds that there is an infringement it may impose a lump sum or penalty payment on the Member State concerned not exceeding the amount specified by the Commission. The payment obligation shall take effect on the date set by the Court in its judgment.

ARTICLE III-363

European laws and regulations of the Council may give the Court of Justice of the European Union unlimited jurisdiction with regard to the penalties provided for in them.

ARTICLE III-364

Without prejudice to the other provisions of the Constitution, a European law may confer on the Court of Justice of the European Union, to the extent that it shall determine, jurisdiction in disputes relating to the application of acts adopted on the basis of the Constitution which create European intellectual property rights.

ARTICLE III-365

1.   The Court of Justice of the European Union shall review the legality of European laws and framework laws, of acts of the Council, of the Commission and of the European Central Bank, other than recommendations and opinions, and of acts of the European Parliament and of the European Council intended to produce legal effects vis-à-vis third parties. It shall also review the legality of acts of bodies, offices or agencies of the Union intended to produce legal effects vis-à-vis third parties.

2.   For the purposes of paragraph 1, the Court of Justice of the European Union shall have jurisdiction in actions brought by a Member State, the European Parliament, the Council or the Commission on grounds of lack of competence, infringement of an essential procedural requirement, infringement of the Constitution or of any rule of law relating to its application, or misuse of powers.

3.   The Court of Justice of the European Union shall have jurisdiction under the conditions laid down in paragraphs 1 and 2 in actions brought by the Court of Auditors, by the European Central Bank and by the Committee of the Regions for the purpose of protecting their prerogatives.

4.   Any natural or legal person may, under the conditions laid down in paragraphs 1 and 2, institute proceedings against an act addressed to that person or which is of direct and individual concern to him or her, and against a regulatory act which is of direct concern to him or her and does not entail implementing measures.

5.   Acts setting up bodies, offices and agencies of the Union may lay down specific conditions and arrangements concerning actions brought by natural or legal persons against acts of these bodies, offices or agencies intended to produce legal effects in relation to them.

6.   The proceedings provided for in this Article shall be instituted within two months of the publication of the act, or of its notification to the plaintiff, or, in the absence thereof, of the day on which it came to the plaintiff's knowledge, as the case may be.

ARTICLE III-366

If the action is well founded, the Court of Justice of the European Union shall declare the act concerned to be void.

However, the Court shall, if it considers this necessary, state which of the effects of the act which it has declared void shall be considered as definitive.

ARTICLE III-367

Should the European Parliament, the European Council, the Council, the Commission or the European Central Bank, in infringement of the Constitution, fail to act, the Member States and the other institutions of the Union may bring an action before the Court of Justice of the European Union to have the infringement established. This Article shall apply, under the same conditions, to bodies, offices and agencies of the Union which fail to act.

The action shall be admissible only if the institution, body, office or agency concerned has first been called upon to act. If, within two months of being so called upon, the institution, body, office or agency concerned has not defined its position, the action may be brought within a further period of two months.

Any natural or legal person may, under the conditions laid down in the first and second paragraphs, complain to the Court that an institution, body, office or agency of the Union has failed to address to that person any act other than a recommendation or an opinion.

ARTICLE III-368

The institution, body, office or agency whose act has been declared void, or whose failure to act has been declared contrary to the Constitution, shall be required to take the necessary measures to comply with the judgment of the Court of Justice of the European Union.

This obligation shall not affect any obligation which may result from the application of the second paragraph of Article III-431.

ARTICLE III-369

The Court of Justice of the European Union shall have jurisdiction to give preliminary rulings concerning:

(a)   the interpretation of the Constitution;

(b)   the validity and interpretation of acts of the institutions, bodies, offices and agencies of the Union.

Where such a question is raised before any court or tribunal of a Member State, that court or tribunal may, if it considers that a decision on the question is necessary to enable it to give judgment, request the Court to give a ruling thereon.

Where any such question is raised in a case pending before a court or tribunal of a Member State against whose decisions there is no judicial remedy under national law, that court or tribunal shall bring the matter before the Court.

If such a question is raised in a case pending before a court or tribunal of a Member State with regard to a person in custody, the Court shall act with the minimum of delay.

ARTICLE III-370

The Court of Justice of the European Union shall have jurisdiction in disputes relating to compensation for damage provided for in the second and third paragraphs of Article III-431.

ARTICLE III-371

The Court of Justice shall have jurisdiction to decide on the legality of an act adopted by the European Council or by the Council pursuant to Article I-59 solely at the request of the Member State concerned by a determination of the European Council or of the Council and in respect solely of the procedural stipulations contained in that Article.

Such a request must be made within one month from the date of such determination. The Court shall rule within one month from the date of the request.

ARTICLE III-372

The Court of Justice of the European Union shall have jurisdiction in any dispute between the Union and its servants within the limits and under the conditions laid down in the Staff Regulations of Officials and the Conditions of Employment of other servants of the Union.

ARTICLE III-373

The Court of Justice of the European Union shall, within the limits hereinafter laid down, have jurisdiction in disputes concerning:

(a) the fulfilment by Member States of obligations under the Statute of the European Investment Bank. In this connection, the Board of Directors of the Bank shall enjoy the powers conferred upon the Commission by Article III-360;

(b) measures adopted by the Board of Governors of the European Investment Bank. In this connection, any Member State, the Commission or the Board of Directors of the Bank may institute proceedings under the conditions laid down in Article III-365;

(c) measures adopted by the Board of Directors of the European Investment Bank. Proceedings against such measures may be instituted only by Member States or by the Commission, under the conditions laid down in Article III-365, and solely on the grounds of non-compliance with the procedure provided for in Article 19(2), (5), (6) and (7) of the Statute of the Bank;

(d) the fulfilment by national central banks of obligations under the Constitution and the Statute of the European System of Central Banks and of the European Central Bank. In this connection, the powers of the Governing Council of the European Central Bank in respect of national central banks shall be the same as those conferred upon the Commission in respect of Member States by Article III-360. If the Court of Justice of the European Union finds that a national central bank has failed to fulfil an obligation under the Constitution, that bank shall be required to take the necessary measures to comply with the judgment of the Court.

ARTICLE III-374

The Court of Justice of the European Union shall have jurisdiction to give judgment pursuant to any arbitration clause contained in a contract concluded by or on behalf of the Union, whether that contract be governed by public or private law.

ARTICLE III-375

1.   Save where jurisdiction is conferred on the Court of Justice of the European Union by the Constitution, disputes to which the Union is a party shall not on that ground be excluded from the jurisdiction of the courts or tribunals of the Member States.

2.   Member States undertake not to submit a dispute concerning the interpretation or application of the Constitution to any method of settlement other than those provided for therein.

3.   The Court of Justice shall have jurisdiction in any dispute between Member States which relates to the subject-matter of the Constitution if the dispute is submitted to it under a special agreement between the parties.

ARTICLE III-376

The Court of Justice of the European Union shall not have jurisdiction with respect to Articles I-40 and I-41 and the provisions of Chapter II of Title V concerning the common foreign and security policy and Article III-293 insofar as it concerns the common foreign and security policy.

However, the Court shall have jurisdiction to monitor compliance with Article III-308 and to rule on proceedings, brought in accordance with the conditions laid down in Article III-365(4), reviewing the legality of European decisions providing for restrictive measures against natural or legal persons adopted by the Council on the basis of Chapter II of Title V.

ARTICLE III-377

In exercising its powers regarding the provisions of Sections 4 and 5 of Chapter IV of Title III relating to the area of freedom, security and justice, the Court of Justice of the European Union shall have no jurisdiction to review the validity or proportionality of operations carried out by the police or other law-enforcement services of a Member State or the exercise of the responsibilities incumbent upon Member States with regard to the maintenance of law and order and the safeguarding of internal security.

ARTICLE III-378

Notwithstanding the expiry of the period laid down in Article III-365(6), any party may, in proceedings in which an act of general application adopted by an institution, body, office or agency of the Union is at issue, plead the grounds specified in Article III-365(2) in order to invoke before the Court of Justice of the European Union the inapplicability of that act.

ARTICLE III-379

1.   Actions brought before the Court of Justice of the European Union shall not have suspensory effect. The Court may, however, if it considers that circumstances so require, order that application of the contested act be suspended.

2.   The Court of Justice of the European Union may in any cases before it prescribe any necessary interim measures.

ARTICLE III-380

The judgments of the Court of Justice of the European Union shall be enforceable under the conditions laid down in Article III-401.

ARTICLE III-381

The Statute of the Court of Justice of the European Union shall be laid down in a Protocol.

A European law may amend the provisions of the Statute, with the exception of Title I and Article 64. It shall be adopted either at the request of the Court of Justice and after consultation of the Commission, or on a proposal from the Commission and after consultation of the Court of Justice.

Subsection 6

The European Central Bank

ARTICLE III-382

1.   The Governing Council of the European Central Bank shall comprise the members of the Executive Board of the European Central Bank and the Governors of the national central banks of the Member States without a derogation as referred to in Article III-197.

2.   The Executive Board shall comprise the President, the Vice-President and four other members.

The President, the Vice-President and the other members of the Executive Board shall be appointed by the European Council, acting by a qualified majority, from among persons of recognised standing and professional experience in monetary or banking matters, on a recommendation from the Council and after consulting the European Parliament and the Governing Council of the European Central Bank.

Their term of office shall be eight years and shall not be renewable.

Only nationals of Member States may be members of the Executive Board.

ARTICLE III-383

1. The President of the Council and a member of the Commission may participate, without having the right to vote, in meetings of the Governing Council of the European Central Bank.

The President of the Council may submit a motion for deliberation to the Governing Council of the European Central Bank.

2. The President of the European Central Bank shall be invited to participate in meetings of the Council when it is discussing matters relating to the objectives and tasks of the European System of Central Banks.

3. The European Central Bank shall address an annual report on the activities of the European System of Central Banks and on the monetary policy of both the previous and the current year to the European Parliament, the European Council, the Council and the Commission. The President of the European Central Bank shall present this report to the European Parliament, which may hold a general debate on that basis, and to the Council.

The President of the European Central Bank and the other members of the Executive Board may, at the request of the European Parliament or on their own initiative, be heard by the competent bodies of the European Parliament.

Subsection 7

The Court of Auditors

ARTICLE III-384

1. The Court of Auditors shall examine the accounts of all revenue and expenditure of the Union. It shall also examine the accounts of all revenue and expenditure of any body, office or agency set up by the Union insofar as the instrument establishing that body, office or agency does not preclude such examination.

The Court of Auditors shall provide the European Parliament and the Council with a statement of assurance as to the reliability of the accounts and the legality and regularity of the underlying transactions which shall be published in the Official Journal of the European Union. This statement may be supplemented by specific assessments for each major area of Union activity.

2. The Court of Auditors shall examine whether all revenue has been received and all expenditure incurred in a lawful and regular manner and whether the financial management has been sound. In doing so, it shall report in particular on any cases of irregularity.

The audit of revenue shall be carried out on the basis of the amounts established as due and the amounts actually paid to the Union.

The audit of expenditure shall be carried out on the basis both of commitments undertaken and payments made.

These audits may be carried out before the closure of accounts for the financial year in question.

3.   The audit shall be based on records and, if necessary, performed on the spot in the other institutions, or on the premises of any body, office or agency which manages revenue or expenditure on behalf of the Union and in the Member States, including on the premises of any natural or legal person in receipt of payments from the budget. In the Member States the audit shall be carried out in liaison with national audit bodies or, if these do not have the necessary powers, with the competent national departments. The Court of Auditors and the national audit bodies of the Member States shall cooperate in a spirit of trust while maintaining their independence. These bodies or departments shall inform the Court of Auditors whether they intend to take part in the audit.

The other institutions, any bodies, offices or agencies managing revenue or expenditure on behalf of the Union, any natural or legal person in receipt of payments from the budget, and the national audit bodies or, if these do not have the necessary powers, the competent national departments, shall forward to the Court of Auditors, at its request, any document or information necessary to carry out its task.

In respect of the European Investment Bank's activity in managing Union revenue and expenditure, rights of access by the Court of Auditors to information held by the Bank shall be governed by an agreement between the Court of Auditors, the Bank and the Commission. In the absence of an agreement, the Court of Auditors shall nevertheless have access to information necessary for the audit of Union expenditure and revenue managed by the Bank.

4.   The Court of Auditors shall draw up an annual report after the close of each financial year. It shall be forwarded to the other institutions and shall be published, together with the replies of these institutions to the observations of the Court of Auditors, in the Official Journal of the European Union.

The Court of Auditors may also, at any time, submit observations, particularly in the form of special reports, on specific questions and deliver opinions at the request of one of the other institutions.

It shall adopt its annual reports, special reports or opinions by a majority of its component members. However, it may establish internal chambers in order to adopt certain categories of reports or opinions under the conditions laid down by its Rules of Procedure.

It shall assist the European Parliament and the Council in exercising their powers of control over the implementation of the budget.

It shall adopt its Rules of Procedure. Those rules shall require the consent of the Council .

ARTICLE III-385

1.   The members of the Court of Auditors shall be chosen from among persons who belong or have belonged in their respective States to external audit bodies or who are especially qualified for this office. Their independence must be beyond doubt.

2.   The members of the Court of Auditors shall be appointed for a term of six years. Their term of office shall be renewable. The Council shall adopt a European decision establishing the list of members drawn up in accordance with the proposals made by each Member State. It shall act after consulting the European Parliament.

The members of the Court of Auditors shall elect their President from among their number for a term of three years. He or she may be re-elected.

3.   In the performance of their duties, members of the Court of Auditors shall neither seek nor take instructions from any government or from any other body. They shall refrain from any action incompatible with their duties.

4.   Members of the Court of Auditors shall not, during their term of office, engage in any other occupation, whether gainful or not. When entering upon their duties they shall give a solemn undertaking that, both during and after their term of office, they will respect the obligations arising therefrom and in particular their duty to behave with integrity and discretion as regards the acceptance, after they have ceased to hold office, of certain appointments or benefits.

5.   Apart from normal replacement, or death, the duties of a member of the Court of Auditors shall end when he or she resigns, or is compulsorily retired by a ruling of the Court of Justice pursuant to paragraph 6.

The vacancy thus caused shall be filled for the remainder of the member's term of office.

Save in the case of compulsory retirement, members of the Court of Auditors shall remain in office until they have been replaced.

6.   A member of the Court of Auditors may be deprived of his or her office or of his or her right to a pension or other benefits in its stead only if the Court of Justice, at the request of the Court of Auditors, finds that he or she no longer fulfils the requisite conditions or meets the obligations arising from his or her office.

SECTION 2

THE UNION'S ADVISORY BODIES

Subsection 1

The Committee of the Regions

ARTICLE III-386

The number of members of the Committee of the Regions shall not exceed 350. The Council, acting unanimously on a proposal from the Commission, shall adopt a European decision determining the Committee's composition.

The members of the Committee and an equal number of alternate members shall be appointed for five years. Their term of office shall be renewable. No member of the Committee shall at the same time be a member of the European Parliament.

The Council shall adopt the European decision establishing the list of members and alternate members drawn up in accordance with the proposals made by each Member State.

When the mandate referred to in Article I-32(2) on the basis of which they were proposed comes to an end, the term of office of members of the Committee shall terminate automatically and they shall then be replaced for the remainder of the said term of office in accordance with the same procedure.

ARTICLE III-387

The Committee of the Regions shall elect its chairman and officers from among its members for a term of two and a half years.

It shall be convened by its chairman at the request of the European Parliament, of the Council or of the Commission. It may also meet on its own initiative.

It shall adopt its Rules of Procedure.

ARTICLE III-388

The Committee of the Regions shall be consulted by the European Parliament, by the Council or by the Commission where the Constitution so provides and in all other cases in which one of these institutions considers it appropriate, in particular those which concern cross-border cooperation.

The European Parliament, the Council or the Commission shall, if it considers it necessary, set the Committee, for the submission of its opinion, a time-limit which shall not be less than one month from the date on which the chairman receives notification to this effect. Upon expiry of the time-limit, the absence of an opinion shall not prevent further action.

Where the Economic and Social Committee is consulted, the Committee of the Regions shall be informed by the European Parliament, the Council or the Commission of the request for an opinion. Where it considers that specific regional interests are involved, the Committee of the Regions may issue an opinion on the matter. It may also issue an opinion on its own initiative.

The opinion of the Committee, together with a record of its proceedings, shall be forwarded to the European Parliament, to the Council and to the Commission.

Subsection 2
The Economic and Social Committee

ARTICLE III-389

The number of members of the Economic and Social Committee shall not exceed 350. The Council, acting unanimously on a proposal from the Commission, shall adopt a European decision determining the Committee's composition.

ARTICLE III-390

The members of the Economic and Social Committee shall be appointed for five years. Their term of office shall be renewable.

The Council shall adopt the European decision establishing the list of members drawn up in accordance with the proposals made by each Member State.

The Council shall act after consulting the Commission. It may obtain the opinion of European bodies which are representative of the various economic and social sectors and of civil society to which the Union's activities are of concern.

ARTICLE III-391

The Economic and Social Committee shall elect its chairman and officers from among its members for a term of two and a half years.

It shall be convened by its chairman at the request of the European Parliament, of the Council or of the Commission. It may also meet on its own initiative.

It shall adopt its Rules of Procedure.

ARTICLE III-392

The Economic and Social Committee shall be consulted by the European Parliament, by the Council or by the Commission where the Constitution so provides. It may be consulted by these institutions in all cases in which they consider it appropriate. It may also issue an opinion on its own initiative.

The European Parliament, the Council or the Commission shall, if it considers it necessary, set the Committee, for the submission of its opinion, a time-limit which shall not be less than one month from the date on which the chairman receives notification to this effect. Upon expiry of the time-limit, the absence of an opinion shall not prevent further action.

The opinion of the Committee, together with a record of its proceedings, shall be forwarded to the European Parliament, to the Council and to the Commission.

SECTION 3

THE EUROPEAN INVESTMENT BANK

ARTICLE III-393

The European Investment Bank shall have legal personality.

Its members shall be the Member States.

The Statute of the European Investment Bank is laid down in a Protocol.

A European law of the Council may amend the Statute of the European Investment Bank. The Council shall act unanimously, either at the request of the European Investment Bank and after consulting the European Parliament and the Commission, or on a proposal from the Commission and after consulting the European Parliament and the European Investment Bank.

ARTICLE III-394

The task of the European Investment Bank shall be to contribute, by having recourse to the capital markets and utilising its own resources, to the balanced and steady development of the internal market in the Union's interest. For this purpose the European Investment Bank shall, operating on a non-profit-making basis, in particular grant loans and give guarantees which facilitate the financing of the following projects in all sectors of the economy:

(a)   projects for developing less-developed regions;

(b)   projects for modernising or converting undertakings or for developing fresh activities called for by the establishment or functioning of the internal market, where these projects are of such a size or nature that they cannot be entirely financed by the various means available in the individual Member States;

(c)   projects of common interest to several Member States which are of such a size or nature that they cannot be entirely financed by the various means available in the individual Member States.

In carrying out its task, the European Investment Bank shall facilitate the financing of investment programmes in conjunction with assistance from the Structural Funds and other Union financial instruments.

SECTION 4

PROVISIONS COMMON TO UNION INSTITUTIONS, BODIES, OFFICES AND AGENCIES

ARTICLE III-395

1.   Where, pursuant to the Constitution, the Council acts on a proposal from the Commission, it may amend that proposal only by acting unanimously, except in the cases referred to in Articles I-55, I-56, III-396(10) and (13), III-404 and III-405(2).

2.   As long as the Council has not acted, the Commission may alter its proposal at any time during the procedures leading to the adoption of a Union act.

ARTICLE III-396

1.   Where, pursuant to the Constitution, European laws or framework laws are adopted under the ordinary legislative procedure, the following provisions shall apply.

2.   The Commission shall submit a proposal to the European Parliament and the Council.

First reading

3.   The European Parliament shall adopt its position at first reading and communicate it to the Council.

4.   If the Council approves the European Parliament's position, the act concerned shall be adopted in the wording which corresponds to the position of the European Parliament.

5.   If the Council does not approve the European Parliament's position, it shall adopt its position at first reading and communicate it to the European Parliament.

6.   The Council shall inform the European Parliament fully of the reasons which led it to adopt its position at first reading. The Commission shall inform the European Parliament fully of its position.

Second reading

7.   If, within three months of such communication, the European Parliament:

(a)   approves the Council's position at first reading or has not taken a decision, the act concerned shall be deemed to have been adopted in the wording which corresponds to the position of the Council;

(b)   rejects, by a majority of its component members, the Council's position at first reading, the proposed act shall be deemed not to have been adopted;

(c)   proposes, by a majority of its component members, amendments to the Council's position at first reading, the text thus amended shall be forwarded to the Council and to the Commission, which shall deliver an opinion on those amendments.

8.   If, within three months of receiving the European Parliament's amendments, the Council, acting by a qualified majority:

(a)   approves all those amendments, the act in question shall be deemed to have been adopted;

(b)   does not approve all the amendments, the President of the Council, in agreement with the President of the European Parliament, shall within six weeks convene a meeting of the Conciliation Committee.

9.   The Council shall act unanimously on the amendments on which the Commission has delivered a negative opinion.

Conciliation

10.   The Conciliation Committee, which shall be composed of the members of the Council or their representatives and an equal number of members representing the European Parliament, shall have the task of reaching agreement on a joint text, by a qualified majority of the members of the Council or their representatives and by a majority of the members representing the European Parliament within six weeks of its being convened, on the basis of the positions of the European Parliament and the Council at second reading.

11.   The Commission shall take part in the Conciliation Committee's proceedings and shall take all necessary initiatives with a view to reconciling the positions of the European Parliament and the Council.

12.   If, within six weeks of its being convened, the Conciliation Committee does not approve the joint text, the proposed act shall be deemed not to have been adopted.

Third reading

13.   If, within that period, the Conciliation Committee approves a joint text, the European Parliament, acting by a majority of the votes cast, and the Council, acting by a qualified majority, shall each have a period of six weeks from that approval in which to adopt the act in question in accordance with the joint text. If they fail to do so, the proposed act shall be deemed not to have been adopted.

14.   The periods of three months and six weeks referred to in this Article shall be extended by a maximum of one month and two weeks respectively at the initiative of the European Parliament or the Council.

Special provisions

15.   Where, in the cases provided for in the Constitution, a law or framework law is submitted to the ordinary legislative procedure on the initiative of a group of Member States, on a recommendation by the European Central Bank, or at the request of the Court of Justice, paragraph 2, the second sentence of paragraph 6, and paragraph 9 shall not apply.

In such cases, the European Parliament and the Council shall communicate the proposed act to the Commission with their positions at first and second readings. The European Parliament or the Council may request the opinion of the Commission throughout the procedure, which the Commission may also deliver on its own initiative. It may also, if it deems it necessary, take part in the Conciliation Committee in accordance with paragraph 11.

ARTICLE III-397

The European Parliament, the Council and the Commission shall consult each other and by common agreement make arrangements for their cooperation. To that end, they may, in compliance with the Constitution, conclude interinstitutional agreements which may be of a binding nature.

ARTICLE III-398

1.   In carrying out their missions, the institutions, bodies, offices and agencies of the Union shall have the support of an open, efficient and independent European administration.

2.   In compliance with the Staff Regulations and the Conditions of Employment adopted on the basis of Article III-427, European laws shall establish provisions to that end.

ARTICLE III-399

1.   The institutions, bodies, offices and agencies of the Union shall ensure transparency in their work and shall, pursuant to Article I-50, determine in their rules of procedure specific provisions for public access to their documents. The Court of Justice of the European Union, the European Central Bank and the European Investment Bank shall be subject to the provisions of Article I-50(3) and to this Article only when exercising their administrative tasks.

2.   The European Parliament and the Council shall ensure publication of the documents relating to the legislative procedures under the terms laid down by the European law referred to in Article I-50(3).

ARTICLE III-400

1.   The Council shall adopt European regulations and decisions determining:

(a)   the salaries, allowances and pensions of the President of the European Council, the President of the Commission, the Union Minister for Foreign Affairs, the members of the Commission, the Presidents, members and Registrars of the Court of Justice of the European Union, and the Secretary-General of the Council;

(b)   the conditions of employment, in particular the salaries, allowances and pensions, of the President and members of the Court of Auditors;

(c)   any payment to be made instead of remuneration to the persons referred to in points (a) and (b).

2.   The Council shall adopt European regulations and decisions determining the allowances of the members of the Economic and Social Committee.

ARTICLE III-401

Acts of the Council, of the Commission or of the European Central Bank which impose a pecuniary obligation on persons other than Member States shall be enforceable.

Enforcement shall be governed by the rules of civil procedure in force in the Member State in the territory of which it is carried out. The order for its enforcement shall be appended to the decision, without other formality than verification of the authenticity of the decision, by the national authority which the government of each Member State shall designate for this purpose and shall make known to the Commission and the Court of Justice of the European Union.

When these formalities have been completed on application by the party concerned, the latter may proceed to enforcement by bringing the matter directly before the competent authority, in accordance with the national law.

Enforcement may be suspended only by a decision of the Court of Justice of the European Union. However, the courts of the country concerned shall have jurisdiction over complaints that enforcement is being carried out in an irregular manner.

CHAPTER II

FINANCIAL PROVISIONS

SECTION 1

THE MULTIANNUAL FINANCIAL FRAMEWORK

ARTICLE III-402

1.　The multiannual financial framework shall be established for a period of at least five years in accordance with Article I-55.

2.　The financial framework shall determine the amounts of the annual ceilings on commitment appropriations by category of expenditure and of the annual ceiling on payment appropriations. The categories of expenditure, limited in number, shall correspond to the Union's major sectors of activity.

3.　The financial framework shall lay down any other provisions required for the annual budgetary procedure to run smoothly.

4.　Where no European law of the Council determining a new financial framework has been adopted by the end of the previous financial framework, the ceilings and other provisions corresponding to the last year of that framework shall be extended until such time as that law is adopted.

5.　Throughout the procedure leading to the adoption of the financial framework, the European Parliament, the Council and the Commission shall take any measure necessary to facilitate the successful completion of the procedure.

SECTION 2

THE UNION'S ANNUAL BUDGET

ARTICLE III-403

The financial year shall run from 1 January to 31 December.

ARTICLE III-404

European laws shall establish the Union's annual budget in accordance with the following provisions:

1.　Each institution shall, before 1 July, draw up estimates of its expenditure for the following financial year. The Commission shall consolidate these estimates in a draft budget which may contain different estimates.

The draft budget shall contain an estimate of revenue and an estimate of expenditure.

2.   The Commission shall submit a proposal containing the draft budget to the European Parliament and to the Council not later than 1 September of the year preceding that in which the budget is to be implemented.

The Commission may amend the draft budget during the procedure until such time as the Conciliation Committee, referred to in paragraph 5, is convened.

3.   The Council shall adopt its position on the draft budget and forward it to the European Parliament not later than 1 October of the year preceding that in which the budget is to be implemented. The Council shall inform the European Parliament in full of the reasons which led it to adopt its position.

4.   If, within forty-two days of such communication, the European Parliament:

(a)   approves the position of the Council, the European law establishing the budget shall be adopted;

(b)   has not taken a decision, the European law establishing the budget shall be deemed to have been adopted;

(c)   adopts amendments by a majority of its component members, the amended draft shall be forwarded to the Council and to the Commission. The President of the European Parliament, in agreement with the President of the Council, shall immediately convene a meeting of the Conciliation Committee. However, if within ten days of the draft being forwarded the Council informs the European Parliament that it has approved all its amendments, the Conciliation Committee shall not meet.

5.   The Conciliation Committee, which shall be composed of the members of the Council or their representatives and an equal number of members representing the European Parliament, shall have the task of reaching agreement on a joint text, by a qualified majority of the members of the Council or their representatives and by a majority of the representatives of the European Parliament within twenty-one days of its being convened, on the basis of the positions of the European Parliament and the Council.

The Commission shall take part in the Conciliation Committee's proceedings and shall take all the necessary initiatives with a view to reconciling the positions of the European Parliament and the Council.

6.   If, within the twenty-one days referred to in paragraph 5, the Conciliation Committee agrees on a joint text, the European Parliament and the Council shall each have a period of fourteen days from the date of that agreement in which to approve the joint text.

7.   If, within the period of fourteen days referred to in paragraph 6:

(a)   the European Parliament and the Council both approve the joint text or fail to take a decision, or if one of these institutions approves the joint text while the other one fails to take a decision, the European law establishing the budget shall be deemed to be definitively adopted in accordance with the joint text, or

(b)   the European Parliament, acting by a majority of its component members, and the Council both reject the joint text, or if one of these institutions rejects the joint text while the other one fails to take a decision, a new draft budget shall be submitted by the Commission, or

(c)   the European Parliament, acting by a majority of its component members, rejects the joint text while the Council approves it, a new draft budget shall be submitted by the Commission, or

(d)   the European Parliament approves the joint text whilst the Council rejects it, the European Parliament may, within fourteen days from the date of the rejection by the Council and acting by a majority of its component members and three-fifths of the votes cast, decide to confirm all or some of the amendments referred to in paragraph 4(c). Where a European Parliament amendment is not confirmed, the position agreed in the Conciliation committee on the budget heading which is the subject of the amendment shall be retained. The European law establishing the budget shall be deemed to be definitively adopted on this basis.

8.   If, within the twenty-one days referred to in paragraph 5, the Conciliation Committee does not agree on a joint text, a new draft budget shall be submitted by the Commission.

9.   When the procedure provided for in this Article has been completed, the President of the European Parliament shall declare that the European law establishing the budget has been definitively adopted.

10.   Each institution shall exercise the powers conferred upon it under this Article in compliance with the Constitution and the acts adopted thereunder, with particular regard to the Union's own resources and the balance between revenue and expenditure.

ARTICLE III-405

1.   If at the beginning of a financial year no European law establishing the budget has been definitively adopted, a sum equivalent to not more than one twelfth of the budget appropriations entered in the chapter in question of the budget for the preceding financial year may be spent each month in respect of any chapter in accordance with the European law referred to in Article III-412; that sum shall not, however, exceed one twelfth of the appropriations provided for in the same chapter of the draft budget.

2.   The Council, on a proposal by the Commission and in compliance with the other conditions laid down in paragraph 1, may adopt a European decision authorising expenditure in excess of one twelfth, in accordance with the European law referred to in Article III-412. The Council shall forward the decision immediately to the European Parliament.

The European decision shall lay down the necessary measures relating to resources to ensure application of this Article, in accordance with the European laws referred to in Article I-54(3) and (4).

It shall enter into force thirty days following its adoption if the European Parliament, acting by a majority of its component members, has not decided to reduce this expenditure within that time-limit.

ARTICLE III-406

In accordance with the conditions laid down by the European law referred to in Article III-412, any appropriations, other than those relating to staff expenditure, that are unexpended at the end of the financial year may be carried forward to the next financial year only.

Appropriations shall be classified under different chapters grouping items of expenditure according to their nature or purpose and subdivided in accordance with the European law referred to in Article III-412.

The expenditure of

–   the European Parliament,

–   the European Council and the Council,

–   the Commission, and

–   the Court of Justice of the European Union

shall be set out in separate sections of the budget, without prejudice to special arrangements for certain common items of expenditure.

SECTION 3

IMPLEMENTATION OF THE BUDGET AND DISCHARGE

ARTICLE III-407

The Commission shall implement the budget in cooperation with the Member States, in accordance with the European law referred to in Article III-412, on its own responsibility and within the limits of the appropriations allocated, having regard to the principles of sound financial management. Member States shall cooperate with the Commission to ensure that the appropriations are used in accordance with those principles.

The European law referred to in Article III-412 shall establish the control and audit obligations of the Member States in the implementation of the budget and the resulting responsibilities. It shall establish the responsibilities and detailed rules for each institution concerning its part in effecting its own expenditure.

Within the budget the Commission may, subject to the limits and conditions laid down by the European law referred to in Article III-412, transfer appropriations from one chapter to another or from one subdivision to another.

ARTICLE III-408

The Commission shall submit annually to the European Parliament and to the Council the accounts of the preceding financial year relating to the implementation of the budget. The Commission shall also forward to them a financial statement of the Union's assets and liabilities.

The Commission shall also submit to the European Parliament and to the Council an evaluation report on the Union's finances based on the results achieved, in particular in relation to the indications given by the European Parliament and the Council pursuant to Article III-409.

ARTICLE III-409

1.   The European Parliament, on a recommendation from the Council, shall give a discharge to the Commission in respect of the implementation of the budget. To this end, the Council and the European Parliament in turn shall examine the accounts, the financial statement and the evaluation report referred to in Article III-408, the annual report by the Court of Auditors together with the replies of the institutions under audit to the observations of the Court of Auditors, the statement of assurance referred to in the second subparagraph of Article III-384(1) and any relevant special reports by the Court of Auditors.

2.   Before giving a discharge to the Commission, or for any other purpose in connection with the exercise of its powers over the implementation of the budget, the European Parliament may ask to hear the Commission give evidence with regard to the execution of expenditure or the operation of financial control systems. The Commission shall submit any necessary information to the European Parliament at the latter's request.

3.   The Commission shall take all appropriate steps to act on the observations in the decisions giving discharge and on other observations by the European Parliament relating to the execution of expenditure, as well as on comments accompanying the recommendations on discharge adopted by the Council.

4.   At the request of the European Parliament or the Council, the Commission shall report on the measures taken in the light of these observations and comments and in particular on the instructions given to the departments which are responsible for the implementation of the budget. These reports shall also be forwarded to the Court of Auditors.

SECTION 4

COMMON PROVISIONS

ARTICLE III-410

The multiannual financial framework and the annual budget shall be drawn up in euro.

ARTICLE III-411

The Commission may, provided it notifies the competent authorities of the Member States concerned, transfer into the currency of one of the Member States its holdings in the currency of another Member State, to the extent necessary to enable them to be used for purposes which come within the scope of the Constitution. The Commission shall as far as possible avoid making such transfers if it possesses cash or liquid assets in the currencies which it needs.

The Commission shall deal with each Member State concerned through the authority designated by that State. In carrying out financial operations the Commission shall employ the services of the bank of issue of the Member State concerned or of any other financial institution approved by that State.

ARTICLE III-412

1.   European laws shall establish:

(a)   the financial rules which determine in particular the procedure to be adopted for establishing and implementing the budget and for presenting and auditing accounts;

(b)   rules providing for checks on the responsibility of financial actors, in particular authorising officers and accounting officers.

Such European laws shall be adopted after consultation of the Court of Auditors.

2.   The Council shall, on a proposal from the Commission, adopt a European regulation laying down the methods and procedure whereby the budget revenue provided under the arrangements relating to the Union's own resources shall be made available to the Commission, and the measures to be applied, if need be, to meet cash requirements. The Council shall act after consulting the European Parliament and the Court of Auditors.

3.   The Council shall act unanimously until 31 December 2006 in all the cases referred to by this Article.

ARTICLE III-413

The European Parliament, the Council and the Commission shall ensure that the financial means are made available to allow the Union to fulfil its legal obligations in respect of third parties.

ARTICLE III-414

Regular meetings between the Presidents of the European Parliament, the Council and the Commission shall be convened, on the initiative of the Commission, under the budgetary procedures referred to in this Chapter. The Presidents shall take all the necessary steps to promote consultation and the reconciliation of the positions of the institutions over which they preside in order to facilitate the implementation of this Chapter.

SECTION 5

COMBATING FRAUD

ARTICLE III-415

1.   The Union and the Member States shall counter fraud and any other illegal activities affecting the Union's financial interests through measures taken in accordance with this Article. These measures shall act as a deterrent and be such as to afford effective protection in the Member States and in all the Union's institutions, bodies, offices and agencies.

2.   Member States shall take the same measures to counter fraud affecting the Union's financial interests as they take to counter fraud affecting their own financial interests.

3.   Without prejudice to other provisions of the Constitution, the Member States shall coordinate their action aimed at protecting the Union's financial interests against fraud. To this end they shall organise, together with the Commission, close and regular cooperation between the competent authorities.

4.   European laws or framework laws shall lay down the necessary measures in the fields of the prevention of and fight against fraud affecting the Union's financial interests with a view to affording effective and equivalent protection in the Member States and in all the Union's institutions, bodies, offices and agencies. They shall be adopted after consultation of the Court of Auditors.

5.   The Commission, in cooperation with Member States, shall each year submit to the European Parliament and to the Council a report on the measures taken for the implementation of this Article.

CHAPTER III

ENHANCED COOPERATION

ARTICLE III-416

Any enhanced cooperation shall comply with the Constitution and the law of the Union.

Such cooperation shall not undermine the internal market or economic, social and territorial cohesion. It shall not constitute a barrier to or discrimination in trade between Member States, nor shall it distort competition between them.

ARTICLE III-417

Any enhanced cooperation shall respect the competences, rights and obligations of those Member States which do not participate in it. Those Member States shall not impede its implementation by the participating Member States.

ARTICLE III-418

1.   When enhanced cooperation is being established, it shall be open to all Member States, subject to compliance with any conditions of participation laid down by the European authorising decision. It shall also be open to them at any other time, subject to compliance with the acts already adopted within that framework, in addition to any such conditions.

The Commission and the Member States participating in enhanced cooperation shall ensure that they promote participation by as many Member States as possible.

2.   The Commission and, where appropriate, the Union Minister for Foreign Affairs shall keep the European Parliament and the Council regularly informed regarding developments in enhanced cooperation.

ARTICLE III-419

1.   Member States which wish to establish enhanced cooperation between themselves in one of the areas covered by the Constitution, with the exception of fields of exclusive competence and the common foreign and security policy, shall address a request to the Commission, specifying the scope and objectives of the enhanced cooperation proposed. The Commission may submit a proposal to the Council to that effect. In the event of the Commission not submitting a proposal, it shall inform the Member States concerned of the reasons for not doing so.

Authorisation to proceed with enhanced cooperation shall be granted by a European decision of the Council, which shall act on a proposal from the Commission and after obtaining the consent of the European Parliament.

2.   The request of the Member States which wish to establish enhanced cooperation between themselves within the framework of the common foreign and security policy shall be addressed to the Council. It shall be forwarded to the Union Minister for Foreign Affairs, who shall give an opinion on whether the enhanced cooperation proposed is consistent with the Union's common foreign and security policy, and to the Commission, which shall give its opinion in particular on whether the enhanced cooperation proposed is consistent with other Union policies. It shall also be forwarded to the European Parliament for information.

Authorisation to proceed with enhanced cooperation shall be granted by a European decision of the Council acting unanimously.

ARTICLE III-420

1.   Any Member State which wishes to participate in enhanced cooperation in progress in one of the areas referred to in Article III-419(1) shall notify its intention to the Council and the Commission.

The Commission shall, within four months of the date of receipt of the notification, confirm the participation of the Member State concerned. It shall note where necessary that the conditions of participation have been fulfilled and shall adopt any transitional measures necessary with regard to the application of the acts already adopted within the framework of enhanced cooperation.

However, if the Commission considers that the conditions of participation have not been fulfilled, it shall indicate the arrangements to be adopted to fulfil those conditions and shall set a deadline for re-examining the request. On the expiry of that deadline, it shall re-examine the request, in accordance with the procedure set out in the second subparagraph. If the Commission considers that the conditions of participation have still not been met, the Member State concerned may refer the matter to the Council, which shall decide on the request. The Council shall act in accordance with Article I-44(3). It may also adopt the transitional measures referred to in the second subparagraph on a proposal from the Commission.

2.   Any Member State which wishes to participate in enhanced cooperation in progress in the framework of the common foreign and security policy shall notify its intention to the Council, the Union Minister for Foreign Affairs and the Commission.

The Council shall confirm the participation of the Member State concerned, after consulting the Union Minister for Foreign Affairs and after noting, where necessary, that the conditions of participation have been fulfilled. The Council, on a proposal from the Union Minister for Foreign Affairs, may also adopt any transitional measures necessary with regard to the application of the acts already adopted within the framework of enhanced cooperation. However, if the Council considers that the conditions of participation have not been fulfilled, it shall indicate the arrangements to be adopted to fulfil those conditions and shall set a deadline for re-examining the request for participation.

For the purposes of this paragraph, the Council shall act unanimously and in accordance with Article I-44(3).

ARTICLE III-421

Expenditure resulting from implementation of enhanced cooperation, other than administrative costs entailed for the institutions, shall be borne by the participating Member States, unless all members of the Council, acting unanimously after consulting the European Parliament, decide otherwise.

ARTICLE III-422

1.   Where a provision of the Constitution which may be applied in the context of enhanced cooperation stipulates that the Council shall act unanimously, the Council, acting unanimously in accordance with the arrangements laid down in Article I-44(3), may adopt a European decision stipulating that it will act by a qualified majority.

2.   Where a provision of the Constitution which may be applied in the context of enhanced cooperation stipulates that the Council shall adopt European laws or framework laws under a special legislative procedure, the Council, acting unanimously in accordance with the arrangements laid down in Article I-44(3), may adopt a European decision stipulating that it will act under the ordinary legislative procedure. The Council shall act after consulting the European Parliament.

3.   Paragraphs 1 and 2 shall not apply to decisions having military or defence implications.

ARTICLE III-423

The Council and the Commission shall ensure the consistency of activities undertaken in the context of enhanced cooperation and the consistency of such activities with the policies of the Union, and shall cooperate to that end.

TITLE VII

COMMON PROVISIONS

ARTICLE III-424

Taking account of the structural economic and social situation of Guadeloupe, French Guiana, Martinique, Réunion, the Azores, Madeira and the Canary Islands, which is compounded by their remoteness, insularity, small size, difficult topography and climate, economic dependence on a few products, the permanence and combination of which severely restrain their development, the Council, on a proposal from the Commission, shall adopt European laws, framework laws, regulations and decisions aimed, in particular, at laying down the conditions of application of the Constitution to those regions, including common policies. It shall act after consulting the European Parliament.

The acts referred to in the first paragraph concern in particular areas such as customs and trade policies, fiscal policy, free zones, agriculture and fisheries policies, conditions for supply of raw materials and essential consumer goods, State aids and conditions of access to structural funds and to horizontal Union programmes.

The Council shall adopt the acts referred to in the first paragraph taking into account the special characteristics and constraints of the outermost regions without undermining the integrity and the coherence of the Union legal order, including the internal market and common policies.

ARTICLE III-425

The Constitution shall in no way prejudice the rules in Member States governing the system of property ownership.

ARTICLE III-426

In each of the Member States, the Union shall enjoy the most extensive legal capacity accorded to legal persons under their laws; it may, in particular, acquire or dispose of movable and immovable property and may be a party to legal proceedings. To this end, the Union shall be represented by the Commission. However, the Union shall be represented by each of the institutions, by virtue of their administrative autonomy, in matters relating to their respective operation.

ARTICLE III-427

The Staff Regulations of officials and the Conditions of Employment of other servants of the Union shall be laid down by a European law. It shall be adopted after consultation of the institutions concerned.

ARTICLE III-428

The Commission may, within the limits and under conditions laid down by a European regulation or decision adopted by a simple majority by the Council, collect any information and carry out any checks required for the performance of the tasks entrusted to it.

ARTICLE III-429

1.   Without prejudice to Article 5 of the Protocol on the Statute of the European System of Central Banks and of the European Central Bank, measures for the production of statistics shall be laid down by a European law or framework law where necessary for the performance of the Union's activities.

2.   The production of statistics shall conform to impartiality, reliability, objectivity, scientific independence, cost-effectiveness and statistical confidentiality. It shall not entail excessive burdens on economic operators.

ARTICLE III-430

The members of the Union's institutions, the members of committees, and the officials and other servants of the Union shall be required, even after their duties have ceased, not to disclose information of the kind covered by the obligation of professional secrecy, in particular information about undertakings, their business relations or their cost components.

ARTICLE III-431

The Union's contractual liability shall be governed by the law applicable to the contract in question.

In the case of non-contractual liability, the Union shall, in accordance with the general principles common to the laws of the Member States, make good any damage caused by its institutions or by its servants in the performance of their duties.

Notwithstanding the second paragraph, the European Central Bank shall, in accordance with the general principles common to the laws of the Member States, make good any damage caused by it or by its servants in the performance of their duties.

The personal liability of its servants towards the Union shall be governed by the provisions laid down in their Staff Regulations or in the Conditions of Employment applicable to them.

ARTICLE III-432

The seat of the Union's institutions shall be determined by common accord of the governments of the Member States.

ARTICLE III-433

The Council shall adopt unanimously a European regulation laying down the rules governing the languages of the Union's institutions, without prejudice to the Statute of the Court of Justice of the European Union.

ARTICLE III-434

The Union shall enjoy in the territories of the Member States such privileges and immunities as are necessary for the performance of its tasks, under the conditions laid down in the Protocol on the privileges and immunities of the European Union.

ARTICLE III-435

The rights and obligations arising from agreements concluded before 1 January 1958 or, for acceding States, before the date of their accession, between one or more Member States on the one hand, and one or more third countries on the other, shall not be affected by the Constitution.

To the extent that such agreements are not compatible with the Constitution, the Member State or States concerned shall take all appropriate steps to eliminate the incompatibilities established. Member States shall, where necessary, assist each other to this end and shall, where appropriate, adopt a common attitude.

In applying the agreements referred to in the first paragraph, Member States shall take into account the fact that the advantages accorded under the Constitution by each Member State form an integral part of the Union and are thereby inseparably linked with the creation of institutions on which powers have been conferred by the Constitution and the granting of identical advantages by all the other Member States.

ARTICLE III-436

1.   The Constitution shall not preclude the application of the following rules:

(a)   no Member State shall be obliged to supply information the disclosure of which it considers contrary to the essential interests of its security;

(b)   any Member State may take such measures as it considers necessary for the protection of the essential interests of its security which are connected with the production of or trade in arms, munitions and war material; such measures shall not adversely affect the conditions of competition in the internal market regarding products which are not intended for specifically military purposes.

2.   The Council, on a proposal from the Commission, may unanimously adopt a European decision making changes to the list of 15 April 1958 of the products to which the provisions of paragraph 1(b) apply.

PART IV
GENERAL AND FINAL PROVISIONS

ARTICLE IV-437

Repeal of earlier Treaties

1.   This Treaty establishing a Constitution for Europe shall repeal the Treaty establishing the European Community, the Treaty on European Union and, under the conditions laid down in the Protocol on the acts and treaties having supplemented or amended the Treaty establishing the European Community and the Treaty on European Union, the acts and treaties which have supplemented or amended them, subject to paragraph 2 of this Article.

2.   The Treaties on the Accession:

(a)   of the Kingdom of Denmark, Ireland and the United Kingdom of Great Britain and Northern Ireland;

(b)   of the Hellenic Republic;

(c)   of the Kingdom of Spain and the Portuguese Republic;

(d)   of the Republic of Austria, the Republic of Finland and the Kingdom of Sweden, and

(e)   of the Czech Republic, the Republic of Estonia, the Republic of Cyprus, the Republic of Latvia, the Republic of Lithuania, the Republic of Hungary, the Republic of Malta, the Republic of Poland, the Republic of Slovenia and the Slovak Republic,

shall be repealed.

Nevertheless:

–   the provisions of the Treaties referred to in points (a) to (d) and set out or referred to in the Protocol on the Treaties and Acts of Accession of the Kingdom of Denmark, Ireland and the United Kingdom of Great Britain and Northern Ireland, of the Hellenic Republic, of the Kingdom of Spain and the Portuguese Republic, and of the Republic of Austria, the Republic of Finland and the Kingdom of Sweden shall remain in force and their legal effects shall be preserved in accordance with that Protocol,

–   the provisions of the Treaty referred to in point (e) and which are set out or referred to in the Protocol on the Treaty and Act of Accession of the Czech Republic, the Republic of Estonia, the Republic of Cyprus, the Republic of Latvia, the Republic of Lithuania, the Republic of Hungary, the Republic of Malta, the Republic of Poland, the Republic of Slovenia and the Slovak Republic shall remain in force and their legal effects shall be preserved in accordance with that Protocol.

ARTICLE IV-438

Succession and legal continuity

1.   The European Union established by this Treaty shall be the successor to the European Union established by the Treaty on European Union and to the European Community.

2.   Until new provisions have been adopted in implementation of this Treaty or until the end of their term of office, the institutions, bodies, offices and agencies existing on the date of the entry into force of this Treaty shall, subject to Article IV-439, exercise their powers within the meaning of this Treaty in their composition on that date.

3.   The acts of the institutions, bodies, offices and agencies adopted on the basis of the treaties and acts repealed by Article IV-437 shall remain in force. Their legal effects shall be preserved until those acts are repealed, annulled or amended in implementation of this Treaty. The same shall apply to agreements concluded between Member States on the basis of the treaties and acts repealed by Article IV-437.

The other components of the *acquis* of the Community and of the Union existing at the time of the entry into force of this Treaty, in particular the interinstitutional agreements, decisions and agreements arrived at by the Representatives of the Governments of the Member States, meeting within the Council, the agreements concluded by the Member States on the functioning of the Union or of the Community or linked to action by the Union or by the Community, the declarations, including those made in the context of intergovernmental conferences, as well as the resolutions or other positions adopted by the European Council or the Council and those relating to the Union or to the Community adopted by common accord by the Member States, shall also be preserved until they have been deleted or amended.

4.   The case law of the Court of Justice of the European Communities and of the Court of First Instance on the interpretation and application of the treaties and acts repealed by Article IV-437, as well as of the acts and conventions adopted for their application, shall remain, mutatis mutandis, the source of interpretation of Union law and in particular of the comparable provisions of the Constitution.

5.   Continuity in administrative and legal procedures commenced prior to the date of entry into force of this Treaty shall be ensured in compliance with the Constitution. The institutions, bodies, offices and agencies responsible for those procedures shall take all appropriate measures to that effect.

ARTICLE IV-439

Transitional provisions relating to certain institutions

The transitional provisions relating to the composition of the European Parliament, to the definition of a qualified majority in the European Council and in the Council, including those cases where not all members of the European Council or Council vote, and to the composition of the Commission, including the Union Minister for Foreign Affairs, shall be laid down in the Protocol on the transitional provisions relating to the institutions and bodies of the Union.

ARTICLE IV-440

Scope

1.   This Treaty shall apply to the Kingdom of Belgium, the Czech Republic, the Kingdom of Denmark, the Federal Republic of Germany, the Republic of Estonia, the Hellenic Republic, the Kingdom of Spain, the French Republic, Ireland, the Italian Republic, the Republic of Cyprus, the Republic of Latvia, the Republic of Lithuania, the Grand Duchy of Luxembourg, the Republic of Hungary, the Republic of Malta, the Kingdom of the Netherlands, the Republic of Austria, the Republic of Poland, the Portuguese Republic, the Republic of Slovenia, the Slovak Republic, the Republic of Finland, the Kingdom of Sweden and the United Kingdom of Great Britain and Northern Ireland.

2.   This Treaty shall apply to Guadeloupe, French Guiana, Martinique, Réunion, the Azores, Madeira and the Canary Islands in accordance with Article III-424.

3.   The special arrangements for association set out in Title IV of Part III shall apply to the overseas countries and territories listed in Annex II.

This Treaty shall not apply to overseas countries and territories having special relations with the United Kingdom of Great Britain and Northern Ireland which are not included in that list.

4.   This Treaty shall apply to the European territories for whose external relations a Member State is responsible.

5.   This Treaty shall apply to the Åland Islands with the derogations which originally appeared in the Treaty referred to in Article IV-437(2)(d) and which have been incorporated in Section 5 of Title V of the Protocol on the Treaties and Acts of Accession of the Kingdom of Denmark, Ireland and the United Kingdom of Great Britain and Northern Ireland, of the Hellenic Republic, of the Kingdom of Spain and the Portuguese Republic, and of the Republic of Austria, the Republic of Finland and the Kingdom of Sweden.

6.   Notwithstanding paragraphs 1 to 5:

(a)   this Treaty shall not apply to the Faeroe Islands;

(b)   this Treaty shall apply to Akrotiri and Dhekelia, the sovereign base areas of the United Kingdom of Great Britain and Northern Ireland in Cyprus, only to the extent necessary to ensure the implementation of the arrangements originally provided for in the Protocol on the Sovereign Base Areas of the United Kingdom of Great Britain and Northern Ireland in Cyprus, annexed to the Act of Accession which is an integral part of the Treaty referred to in Article IV-437(2)(e), and which have been incorporated in Title III of Part II of the Protocol on the Treaty and Act of Accession of the Czech Republic, the Republic of Estonia, the Republic of Cyprus, the Republic of Latvia, the Republic of Lithuania, the Republic of Hungary, the Republic of Malta, the Republic of Poland, the Republic of Slovenia and the Slovak Republic;

(c)   this Treaty shall apply to the Channel Islands and the Isle of Man only to the extent necessary to ensure the implementation of the arrangements for those islands originally set out in the Treaty referred to in Article IV-437(2)(a), and which have been incorporated in Section 3 of Title II of the Protocol on the Treaties and Acts of Accession of the Kingdom of Denmark, Ireland and the United Kingdom of Great Britain and Northern

Ireland, of the Hellenic Republic, of the Kingdom of Spain and the Portuguese Republic, and of the Republic of Austria, the Republic of Finland and the Kingdom of Sweden.

7. The European Council may, on the initiative of the Member State concerned, adopt a European decision amending the status, with regard to the Union, of a Danish, French or Netherlands country or territory referred to in paragraphs 2 and 3. The European Council shall act unanimously after consulting the Commission.

ARTICLE IV-441

Regional unions

This Treaty shall not preclude the existence or completion of regional unions between Belgium and Luxembourg, or between Belgium, Luxembourg and the Netherlands, to the extent that the objectives of these regional unions are not attained by application of the said Treaty.

ARTICLE IV-442

Protocols and Annexes

The Protocols and Annexes to this Treaty shall form an integral part thereof.

ARTICLE IV-443

Ordinary revision procedure

1. The government of any Member State, the European Parliament or the Commission may submit to the Council proposals for the amendment of this Treaty. These proposals shall be submitted to the European Council by the Council and the national Parliaments shall be notified.

2. If the European Council, after consulting the European Parliament and the Commission, adopts by a simple majority a decision in favour of examining the proposed amendments, the President of the European Council shall convene a Convention composed of representatives of the national Parliaments, of the Heads of State or Government of the Member States, of the European Parliament and of the Commission. The European Central Bank shall also be consulted in the case of institutional changes in the monetary area. The Convention shall examine the proposals for amendments and shall adopt by consensus a recommendation to a conference of representatives of the governments of the Member States as provided for in paragraph 3.

The European Council may decide by a simple majority, after obtaining the consent of the European Parliament, not to convene a Convention should this not be justified by the extent of the proposed amendments. In the latter case, the European Council shall define the terms of reference for a conference of representatives of the governments of the Member States.

3. A conference of representatives of the governments of the Member States shall be convened by the President of the Council for the purpose of determining by common accord the amendments to be made to this Treaty.

The amendments shall enter into force after being ratified by all the Member States in accordance with their respective constitutional requirements.

4.   If, two years after the signature of the treaty amending this Treaty, four fifths of the Member States have ratified it and one or more Member States have encountered difficulties in proceeding with ratification, the matter shall be referred to the European Council.

ARTICLE IV-444

Simplified revision procedure

1.   Where Part III provides for the Council to act by unanimity in a given area or case, the European Council may adopt a European decision authorising the Council to act by a qualified majority in that area or in that case.

This paragraph shall not apply to decisions with military implications or those in the area of defence.

2.   Where Part III provides for European laws and framework laws to be adopted by the Council in accordance with a special legislative procedure, the European Council may adopt a European decision allowing for the adoption of such European laws or framework laws in accordance with the ordinary legislative procedure.

3.   Any initiative taken by the European Council on the basis of paragraphs 1 or 2 shall be notified to the national Parliaments. If a national Parliament makes known its opposition within six months of the date of such notification, the European decision referred to in paragraphs 1 or 2 shall not be adopted. In the absence of opposition, the European Council may adopt the decision.

For the adoption of the European decisions referred to in paragraphs 1 and 2, the European Council shall act by unanimity after obtaining the consent of the European Parliament, which shall be given by a majority of its component members.

ARTICLE IV-445

Simplified revision procedure concerning internal Union policies and action

1.   The Government of any Member State, the European Parliament or the Commission may submit to the European Council proposals for revising all or part of the provisions of Title III of Part III on the internal policies and action of the Union.

2.   The European Council may adopt a European decision amending all or part of the provisions of Title III of Part III. The European Council shall act by unanimity after consulting the European Parliament and the Commission, and the European Central Bank in the case of institutional changes in the monetary area.

Such a European decision shall not come into force until it has been approved by the Member States in accordance with their respective constitutional requirements.

3.   The European decision referred to in paragraph 2 shall not increase the competences conferred on the Union in this Treaty.

ARTICLE IV-446

Duration

This Treaty is concluded for an unlimited period.

ARTICLE IV-447

Ratification and entry into force

1.   This Treaty shall be ratified by the High Contracting Parties in accordance with their respective constitutional requirements. The instruments of ratification shall be deposited with the Government of the Italian Republic.

2.   This Treaty shall enter into force on 1 November 2006, provided that all the instruments of ratification have been deposited, or, failing that, on the first day of the second month following the deposit of the instrument of ratification by the last signatory State to take this step.

ARTICLE IV-448

Authentic texts and translations

1.   This Treaty, drawn up in a single original in the Czech, Danish, Dutch, English, Estonian, Finnish, French, German, Greek, Hungarian, Irish, Italian, Latvian, Lithuanian, Maltese, Polish, Portuguese, Slovak, Slovenian, Spanish and Swedish languages, the texts in each of these languages being equally authentic, shall be deposited in the archives of the Government of the Italian Republic, which will transmit a certified copy to each of the governments of the other signatory States.

2.   This Treaty may also be translated into any other languages as determined by Member States among those which, in accordance with their constitutional order, enjoy official status in all or part of their territory. A certified copy of such translations shall be provided by the Member States concerned to be deposited in the archives of the Council.